YOUR BRANDING EDGE

YOUR BRANDING EDGE

HOW **PERSONAL BRANDING** CAN TURBOCHARGE YOUR CAREER

Rahna Barthelmess

Beacon Bright Publishing

YOUR BRANDING EDGE: How Personal Branding Can Turbocharge Your Career

©2014 Rahna Barthelmess

No part of this book may be reproduced or transmitted in any form or by any means, electronic or mechanical, including photocopying, recording, or by an information storage and retrieval system—except by a reviewer who may quote brief passages in a review to be printed in a magazine, newspaper, or on the Web—without permission in writing from the Publisher. For information, please contact:

BEACON BRIGHT
PUBLISHING

821 Country Meadow Lane
St. Louis, MO 63141
www.BeaconBrightPublishing.com

All rights reserved.

Initial interior concept by Kay Green • www.greengraphicdesign.biz;
Finalized interior layout by Juanita Dix • www.designjd.net

Initial cover concept by Nadira Vlaun • www.nadiravlaun.com;
Finalized cover design by Morgan Sachs • sachsmorgan.com

ISBN: 978-0-9907358-0-9
Library of Congress Control Number: 2014915280
Website: YourBrandingEdge.com

Contents

Special Thanks ix

Introduction xi

Chapter 1
Why You Should Care About Personal Branding 1

Chapter 2
Your Goals 15

Chapter 3
What is a Personal Brand? 21

Chapter 4
Be Clear 29

Chapter 5
Be Confident 47

Chapter 6
Be Professional 61

Chapter 7
Be True To Your Brand 73

Chapter 8
Be Connected 89

Chapter 9
Be Bold 105

Chapter 10
Be Dynamic 129

Chapter 11
Putting These Principles into Action 151

About the Author 163

This book is designed to provide information in regard to the subject matter covered. It is sold with the understanding that the publisher and author are not engaged in rendering legal, accounting or other professional service. If legal or other expert assistance is required, the services of a competent professional should be sought.

Every effort has been made to make this book as complete and as accurate as possible. Branding is the work of a lifetime, so there is no way to put everything into one volume. In addition, there may be mistakes both typographical and in content; therefore this text should be used only as a general guide and not as the ultimate source of branding or personal branding information.

The purpose of this book is to educate and inspire. The author and Beacon Bright Publishing shall have neither liability nor responsibility to any person or entity with respect to any loss or damage caused or alleged to be caused directly or indirectly by the information contained in this book.

If you do not wish to be bound by the above, you may return this book to the publisher for a full refund.

Our deepest fear is not that we are inadequate.
Our deepest fear is that we are powerful beyond measure.
It is our light, not our darkness, that most frightens us.
We ask ourselves, "Who am I to be brilliant, gorgeous, talented, and fabulous?"
Actually, who are you not to be?

                        Marianne Williamson, author, teacher, and lecturer

SPECIAL THANKS

So many people have influenced the development of this book. Each of these unique personal brands has turbocharged this book into being.

I believe that gratitude lists are important. Here's mine:

- For my clients, for being interested in personal branding. You cannot teach what you do not know. Your questions, your problems, your heartaches and your triumphs shaped and clarified the ideas in this book more than anything else
- For my parents, who nurtured in me a passion for creativity and innovation, as well as an understanding of the value of persisting until I found "just the right word"
- For the best virtual assistant and friend Holly Koziol
- For the rest of my family, particularly my sister, who encouraged me to do "just one more thing," my brother, who feeds my entrepreneurial spirit, and my uncle, who tolerated every branding discussion
- For my husband's endless patience and for my children, who roll their eyes as we discuss "life lessons" and love me anyway
- For everyone who contributed to the development of the book – from Nadira Vlaun's branding and cover design ideas; to Kay Green's beautiful interior layout; to Morgan Sachs' unique blend of strategy and creativity; to Nancy Simons for editorial tenacity; to Kristen Eckstein and her team for taking this book to actual execution
- For D'vorah Lansky for her unique combination of emotional encouragement and practical tips and tools
- For Kathy McAfee, perennial business partner and personal branding pal
- For Erin Wolfman May, cheerleader extraordinaire

Thank you all for helping me find my branding edge.

INTRODUCTION

Find out who you are and then be that on purpose.

—Dolly Parton

This book is all about you and your career. You picked up this book because you are looking for your branding edge, an advantage that will allow you to "turbocharge your career." But what does that mean?

A turbocharger on a racecar sucks air into the engine and forces it into the combustion chamber at an extremely high velocity. When you hear the high-pitched whine of an Indy 500 racecar engine as it goes by, you are hearing the turbocharger.

And what do you get when you turbocharge an engine?

Power and speed.

A turbocharger helps an engine achieve greater efficiency and more power, and that makes the car go faster.

This book is about helping you get the same thing from your career—power and speed. Your branding edge is the advantage that comes from understanding the nuances of your personal brand and the critical role it plays in advancing your career. Your personal brand acts as a turbocharger, pulling in what is unique about you to create maximum efficiency and more power. If you want to push forward in your career, find more clients, get promoted, do more meaningful work, get a raise, land that dream job, earn that bonus, and be recognized for the contributions you can make, then you are looking for *Your Branding Edge*.

Get to Work Actively Managing Your Brand

This book requires something of you. It requires action. You must do something. Those who put these ideas into action most quickly will see the most benefit. A presentation coach once told me to make sure that I put clear emphasis on my key message, so let me make sure that I am clear. My main message is that *you need to actively manage your personal brand* in order to maximize your potential and turbocharge your career.

> **Actively Manage Your Personal Brand**

There are lots of books with personality tests, leadership tests, or career tests. Books that will help you discover what your purpose is, tap into your passions, and find out who you are. The difference between those books and the one you are holding in your hands is that this book is more about encouraging you to take action. It's not enough just to know who you are; you have to do something with that. It's not enough for you to passively read this book. If you truly want to turbocharge your career, you must take action. You need to let other people know who you are. Don't just sit there and let your career happen to you! Do something about it! *Make* it happen!

This book is meant to be used. It should be dog-eared and tattered by the time you are done with it; my mother would call it a "well-loved book." In order to facilitate an action orientation, I've included exercises and action steps for you to take throughout the course of reading this book. It may be helpful to you to read through the book first, then come back to do the exercises. But let me be clear: *This book is meant to stir you to action!* These guided exercises will help you draw out your personal brand and strategize an action plan to highlight that brand.

I have also highlighted some online resources to assist you on this journey. By the time you have finished this book, you will have a complete action plan for richly expressing your personal brand to achieve the greatest impact on your career. This critical information can then be distilled into a one-page personal branding action plan. If you fully engage in this book, you can achieve amazing results.

I realize that some people may pick up this book or download it just to have an interesting read on the plane ride home. Others will want to dive in completely and immerse themselves in the work by downloading a workbook and other materials from YourBrandingEdge.com/BookExtras. If you are looking for a quick read, print out your branding edge action plan template, read straight through and simply fill out the action plan. If you are looking for a deeper exploration to turbocharge your career, download the full workbook and take the time to do *all* the exercises to help you craft a highly refined personal branding action plan. In my branding work, I have developed strategies in (literally) six minutes, six months, or six years. Obviously, the more time and energy you devote to building the plan, the more confidence you will have in the accuracy and effectiveness of that plan.

The concepts in this book are not new; any marketer will recognize these as classic best practices. The purpose of this book, however, is to do more than just share best practices. I will show you how to *apply* these practices to your life. If you are a student just beginning to think about making your mark in the professional world, these concepts may be new to you. If you've stagnated in your job, this book will help you map a path to reinvigorate your passion for life and perhaps empower you to reimagine your career. If you're a professional looking to move into the upper echelon of your business world, many of these concepts will seem obvious. You may want to use this book as a reminder to help you get back to the basics. Once you are able to master the seven principles of personal branding, you will discover your branding edge.

This book is filled with stories of others who have learned how to inject new energy into their own careers. For several years, I have been developing and delivering a program to help people strengthen their personal brands in order to expand their career opportunities; make bigger contributions to their companies, their industries, and their organizations; and do more personally meaningful work. Throughout this book, you will hear stories that

> *I am my own experiment.*
> *I am my own work of art.*
> —Madonna, singer/songwriter, business woman, cultural icon

show the amazing results that come from putting these strategies into action. You'll read about a woman who was (finally!) promoted to vice president of her company, a college sophomore who landed a killer internship in the field of her dreams, a full scholarship NCAA athlete who followed her dream to become an artist, and an insurance executive who was promoted (twice!) right in the middle of the worst recession in the last seventy-five years. These strategies work, whether you are an entrepreneur trying to grow your own business, a corporate manager stuck in a lifeless job you no longer have passion for, or a college graduate or job seeker facing a saturated job market.

I'm sharing these amazing stories with you to illustrate each of the individual strategies and to inspire you to reach your career goals. Wherever you are in your career, this book will take you to the next level. Even if you implement just one of the strategies, you will see momentum and progress in your career.

And what if you implement them all? Just ask Christine Kalafus, owner of Stitch LLC and creator of couture windows in country homes throughout Connecticut. This insurance agent turned entrepreneur built a thriving business due to her steadfast attention to implementing all of these strategies and *actively managing* her personal brand. You will read about Christine throughout the book in the sidebar boxes of "Christine's story," included in each chapter.

The classic principles I'll share in this book have helped businesses grow and expand for years, but now we're going to apply those principles for your benefit. I have spent my professional career building brands and have learned from some of the greatest marketers of our time. Branding can be an unbelievably powerful tool; it forges titanium-strength bonds with people and moves them to effective action. And we can put it to use for you. Branding is the reason fans stand out in the cold overnight to get a new iPhone, and branding is the reason toilet paper can make someone a millionaire. We're going to use branding to turbocharge your career.

Come Back Again and Again

You will want to revisit the concepts in this book over and over again, because the messages contained here will have different meaning for you at different times in your career. Building your personal brand is the work of a lifetime, not the work of a few hours spent with a book. *Enjoy the process*, take time and delight in all of the different discoveries you make about yourself. This book will take you through a process of understanding who you are, and, more importantly, you'll identify who you want to be and map out a path to be what you want to be, no matter what that is.

Are you ready to find your branding edge? Let's turbocharge your career!

GET YOUR EDGE
Begin to turbocharge your career today!

> To get the most out of this book, download your branding edge action plan right now with all the exercises and questions at YourBrandingEdge.com/BookExtras so that you can do the written exercises as you go along.

Chapter 1

WHY YOU SHOULD CARE ABOUT PERSONAL BRANDING

All of us need to understand the importance of branding. We are CEOs of our own companies: Me Inc. To be in business today, our most important job is to be head marketer for the brand called You.

—Tom Peters, author,
business management consultant,
father of personal branding

Your Personal Brand Matters....a Lot

Here's what I know about you: You are unique. You are one of a kind and have *vital* individual contributions to make to the world. I don't know you personally, so how can I possibly say that?

Because that statement is true for everyone.

Everyone is unique and has individual skills and abilities to give to his or her community, organization, and world. There is no one who possesses all the qualities that make up you in exactly the same way that you do. You are a magnificent bundle of qualities that uniquely combined in a way that is unlike anyone else. You may be funny, organized, fastidious, quirky, bubbly, serious, or any number of other qualities. The way those qualities come together is what makes you, *you*. I don't even have to know you personally to know that you are one of a kind.

That individuality is referred to in corporate circles as your "personal brand." Personal branding is the expression of your individuality, the way you look at things, the way you react to things, the way you approach things. More importantly, your personal brand is what you are known for; think of it as your reputation. Your personal brand embodies that which you do naturally. Maybe you're funny, smart, laid back, perpetually happy, introspective, analytical, musical, creative or quirky.

Your personal brand is that which you express just by being you. You don't have to think about it; you don't have to work at it. I describe it as something that you do as easily as breathing. The problem for many, though, is that we don't recognize those innate qualities as valuable. We don't honor them as anything special, and often we don't see the genius in our own "ordinary." Your branding edge is about learning to highlight those qualities and put them to work in order to attract more of what you want to do.

We're going to talk about branding throughout this book, but one major concept that will help you turbocharge your career is this: *Brands don't happen by accident.* Professional brand managers get paid to make decisions every day that encourage customers to connect with their brands in various ways. I'm going to ask you to make decisions and *take action* to impact other people's perceptions of your personal brand and to encourage them to connect with you.

You Can Evolve into Anything You Want to Be

Right now, you may find that you possess some great qualities that you would like to enhance, while you likely possess some other qualities that you would like to change. This book provides a path to crafting the personal brand that you want to have. Just as a racecar driver has to know how to get the best performance out of his car, so, too, you need to know how to maximize your potential by tapping into all that is great about you.

This book will help you discover how to tap into your resources to help you eliminate negative traits, strengthen positive traits, and do something amazing with the gifts you have. This book will help you determine who you are and, more importantly, *who you want to be* so that you can go and *be that* on purpose. This book will help you understand how to shape that identity—how to mold it and how to develop it.

> *The most difficult thing is the decision to act; the rest is merely tenacity. The fears are paper tigers. You can do anything you decide to do. You can act to change and control your life; and the procedure, the process, is its own reward.*
> —Amelia Earhart, aviation pioneer

What's in It for You?

There are a few main questions to be answered in this book:
- What is a personal brand, and why should I care?
- What is my personal brand?
- How do I develop and enhance my personal brand?
- How can I best express my personal brand?

Understanding what makes you unique and creating the personal brand you want will dramatically impact your life; watch your career blossom, your relationships grow, and your opportunities expand *exponentially*.

Your Branding Edge

It doesn't matter if you're the head of the company or the summer intern; everyone can benefit from strong personal branding.

At one point, I was working with a group of high-potential top talent as a part of Mass Mutual's executive development program. Each individual in the program had been on a three-year rotation, given a new position every twelve months. My personal branding program was the capstone to that program, allowing the group to synthesize the three years of experience, exposure, and education that they had been given. One woman, Kate Ciriello, went through the program and found that the process of being crystal clear about her personal brand tangibly impacted her career and allowed her to leverage her strengths for the good of the company (and her career). When I spoke with her one year later, she shared this:

> *This training came at a really good time for me. I went from executive development program consultant to director, match to market at a time when a ton of positions were being eliminated throughout the company.*
>
> *In our personal branding work, I identified that I have a unique skill of bringing a sense of clarity to situations and being able to get everyone organized around a specific goal—to get everyone 'rowing the boat in the same direction.' Having identified that as a major part of my personal brand, I was better able to implement that skill in my work. The role I entered was ill defined, a real murky, muddy position that hadn't been given a lot of respect.*

Within a few months, feedback was 'Kate's doing a great job. We really have clarity; we're not confused about what we need to be doing.' That felt great.

Within a few months of my starting, I was able to bring real clarity to the position and end the confusion. I was able to develop the reputation that I felt I deserved. The personal branding work was really valuable because I put into practice the principles we had talked about, and shortly after that, I was promoted again!

Kate understood her own personal brand and acted on that. This made her better able to apply that brand and her own personal gifts to her work. The result? Career promotion, personal happiness and value to the work of the company. Individuals can use branding to really own their gifts and choose jobs and career paths that build on them. Businesses can help their employees to understand their own personal brands in order to better fit workers with the jobs that will benefit from their individual skill sets.

A strong personal brand offers numerous benefits to individuals:

1. A strong personal brand will help delineate and strengthen your fit within an organization or industry.

By understanding what your personal brand brings to an organization, you can see where you fit within the whole. Just as each member of a baseball team has a unique position to play and contributes in very different ways, you have unique skills and abilities to bring to your organization. The catcher provides very different skills and possesses different qualities than the outfielder does, but both are very necessary to the team's success. When you understand your personal brand, you can see where you fit on the team.

2. A strong personal brand will strengthen your position in society.

By expressing your personal brand clearly, you enable others to see where you fit into the organization or community that you are associated with, thus strengthening your position. Personal branding works within the corporate environment or the Little League. It might be your church group, company, or family. When you understand and convey what value you bring, people will perceive you differently.

When I worked with LEGO® toys, I had a colleague, another brand manager, who was simply a fountain of creativity. He didn't have to think about it; he just was creative—all the time. It was as simple for him as breathing, and he loved to express that creativity. If you went to lunch with this guy and casually told him about a project you were working on, you could be guaranteed to come away with a least three new ideas for the best way to approach the challenge. So guess who got invited to every brainstorming session for every product line? Creativity was core to his personal brand.

3. A strong personal brand will increase your value and stature in a group.

Those who have a clear personal brand are seen as people who are very valuable. Strong personal brands make it clear what contributions these people are making and can make in the future. When everyone understands that, that person's stature goes up.

Let's say that Joe is the spreadsheet guru in your office. Joe loves spreadsheets; there's nothing more orderly to him than a perfectly designed, perfectly formatted pivot table. If Joe has a strong personal brand, someone in the office will say, "You know, we have a spreadsheet project coming up. Let's get Joe to do it because he knows all about spreadsheets." And so, Joe's value goes up as he becomes more known for his spreadsheet prowess. So whatever it is that your personal brand is, the more people that know about that, the more your value goes up.

4. A strong personal brand will help you clarify what you stand for, what your purpose is.

When you're clear about your personal brand, you'll understand what your purpose is. You'll know the kinds of things that you want to do, as well as those things that you don't want to do. You will be happier if you are living your purpose, and doing the things you want to be doing. It's a very joyful thing.

5. A strong personal brand will create focus, guide your career, and help you do things "on purpose."

Remember, I want you to *actively* manage your personal brand. Your personal brand serves as your ultimate navigational aid, guiding your career path. It creates focus and guides decision-making. We'll talk more in Chapter 10 about evolving your brand. This is absolutely going to be part of your career, so you'll want to evolve purposefully. Once you put a plan in place about how you want to grow and express your personal brand clearly, you will know what activities you should be involved in, as well as those that you should not be involved in. If a strong business opportunity presents itself to you—an opportunity that would potentially generate a great deal of money for you and your family but would require you to give up who you are, what you stand for, and what you are becoming —you should not take the opportunity. Let it pass! In the end, you would be miserable and you would end up doing a disservice to yourself, your family, and the company.

> *I want to put a dent in the universe.*
> —Steve Jobs, innovator, universe-denter, co-founder of Apple, Inc.

I made this mistake myself, so I know from experience what a disaster compromising your brand can be. As you evolve your brand (or more radically reinvent yourself), you may be tempted to fall back to what is comfortable or known.

Because of my years working on marketing campaigns for LEGO toys, headhunters still call me to talk about jobs in the toy industry. At one point, I accepted a job with another huge iconic brand, one that would be very impressive on my resume and would have provided a comfortable living for my family. While there were many attractive aspects of the job, the work didn't leverage the areas I was interested in growing and the management culture was radically different from what I was looking for. The job focused more on my past but not at all on my future. In addition, the serious cultural conflicts were a struggle for me because of the way the leadership managed people and projects. It became very clear very quickly that this was not a good fit, so I stayed in the job less than a month. At first glance, someone might think that working with a high-profile brand would have "turbocharged my career" but in automotive terms, the move acted like water in the gas tank, distracting me from my real purpose. Let me be clear, however. You should certainly evaluate opportunities that present themselves, but you should not jump at every opportunity that comes your way. There may be some merit to the opportunity—financial gain, career prestige, etc. But if you have to sell your soul to do the job, it will not turbocharge your career. Have a plan for your personal brand (and your career) and be guided by that!

6. A strong personal brand will allow the right people to find you.

People who need what you have to offer will naturally gravitate toward you. You will find that they are seeking what it is that you have to offer. More referrals will happen, more business will come your way, and more like-minded people will find you.

The logo for my branding consultancy, Beacon Marketing, is a lighthouse. I chose that visual on purpose because I believe that your brand is your lighthouse. It is the beacon that shines out to others, calling them to the safe harbor of what you have to offer. You want to make sure that beacon shines as brightly as possible so that all the right people can find you.

And the concept of personal branding works whether you are a corporate division leader or a solopreneur. Within an organization, within your industry, or with your clients, you can become known for certain areas of expertise. Then, the right people will find you—the right clients, the right business partners, the right employees. It may be that you own a company and you need an assistant. If you are known as a very philanthropic person, you will attract people who have the same ideals as you do.

7. A strong personal brand will help you attract opportunities to shine.

If you're doing what you love to do, you will do it well. If you are expressing your innate talents, you will be able to do your job with ease. A turbocharged engine is highly efficient and performs at a very high level. That's why they are used in the world's premier automobiles. When you are expressing your personal brand clearly, you will effortlessly and efficiently perform at very high levels as well. It is fun for me to talk about personal branding all the time, and it's easy to brainstorm ways to help them clarify and express their personal brands. That's just part of my brand. When you express your brand clearly, people will understand your strengths and how these strengths coincide with their needs, and this reinforces and strengthens your personal brand even further.

8. A strong personal brand will enhance your performance and experience.

When you get to do the things you love to do, and do them more often, you get even better at them. Therefore your performance is enhanced and you have stronger experiences. These experiences will strengthen your personal brand even more. It becomes an upward spiral of goodness that keeps strengthening your brand and turbocharging your career. If you're in a corporate environment, you'll be asked to be on task forces that mesh with your strengths, which makes work even more fun. If you have more fun at work, you will be happier and more pleasant to be around. This makes you even more attractive. See how having a strong personal brand can impact your career?

All of this has very tangible results. It can result in a higher salary, more clients, more referrals, or "juicier" projects. Overall, your value goes up as you understand and are able to express your personal brand.

Benefits to the Company

Corporate leaders, you will understand the importance of nurturing and developing individual brands within your group or team to benefit both the individual and your company's bottom line. It is in a company's best interest to have people with strong personal brands working in their organizations. As I talk with corporations about training their workforce in personal branding, some will ask *why* they should develop strong personal brands at all levels of their organization. Strong personal brands are *leadership* brands. In general, individual leadership throughout a company strengthens that company immensely. No one can argue that leadership is important to any company. If you can instill strong personal leadership branding throughout the company, everyone benefits, whether we're talking about the mailroom or the boardroom.

When I work with corporations, I usually start with the corporate brand, then discuss a particular team's brand and what contributions this team makes to the overall company brand. Then we break it down into a discussion of each individual's contribution to the team brand and the company brand. They are all related, and they all contribute to a greater whole.

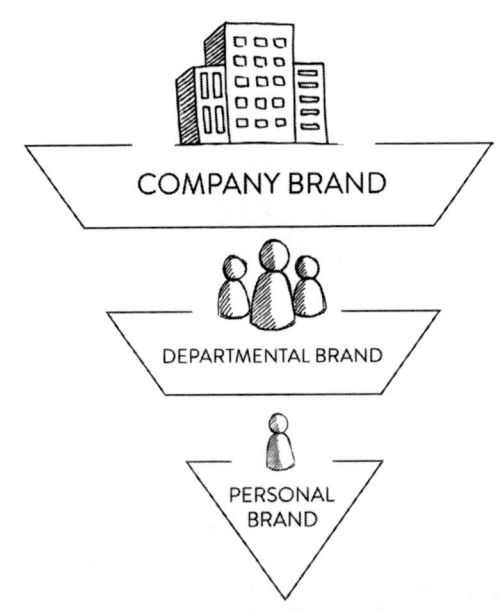

COMPANY BRAND

DEPARTMENTAL BRAND

PERSONAL BRAND

Here are some of the tangible benefits that a company can realize from promoting strong personal brands among its employees:

1. Promoting strong personal brands creates highly motivated self-starters.

When employees understand and promote personal branding, the company gets highly motivated employees who are actively looking for ways to evolve their brands. The way to build an employee's brand is to help him or her add skills, become more professional, and contribute more.

Discussions of personal branding light a fire within each person. It triggers self-motivation and creates a situation where the boss is not telling them how they need to grow. Instead, individual employees are eagerly, actively yearning for more growth, managing themselves, and seeking out areas where they can add more value. What could be better than an employee saying to himself, "How can I add more value at work? What can I do to contribute more?" It will definitely increase personal leadership throughout all levels of the organization.

> *The task of leadership is not to put greatness into humanity, but to elicit it, for the greatness is already there.*
> —John Buchan, British politician, Scottish novelist

2. Promoting strong personal brands improves teamwork and clarifies roles and responsibilities.

There is strong benefit to be realized from a session that would focus on understanding how the various members of the team can blend into a holistic team that leverages the skills each member currently has and identifies the skills members need in order to evolve their brands in a way that benefits everyone. This will meet the company's needs and add to each individual's competencies over time. If you are looking to improve teamwork and workflow, increase productivity and efficiency, then you need to discover your branding edge.

3. Promoting strong personal brands strengthens external perceptions of the company.

Every time department team members talk with someone outside the department, they are creating an impression of that department. When someone in sales talks to a person in purchasing or operations, that person creates an impression. When this person talks to a client or a vendor, again, he or she creates an impression. By having employees focus on what they do well and what the department wants to be known for, they can create a stronger impression of the group—either within the company or within the industry. That will have long-term implications for recruiting efforts, for selling ideas, or for garnering respect with other departments.

4. Promoting strong personal brands provides a framework for career development and succession planning.

Conversations about personal branding express a concern for employee growth. By promoting personal branding explorations in advance of annual individual development planning (or performance management) sessions, it is easy to segue in those discussions to how to build personal brands in the areas that *the company* needs them to focus on.

5. Promoting strong personal brands boosts morale.

People who have clarified their personal brands (and have an action plan in place for how to strengthen it even further) are generally happy. Happy employees are more productive. Morale goes up. Also, when companies promote personal branding, employees will see this as very personally focused. They will see that management cares about their growth, and they will feel that the company is putting them first. There are many different benefits to have corporations work with personal branding. If you are a leader of a team, you are going to want your team to discover their branding edge.

GET YOUR EDGE

1. What challenges would you like this book to solve?

Please answer the following questions:
- What are some of your biggest career challenges today?
- What is keeping your business or career from realizing its full potential?
- As it relates to your career, what keeps you up at night?
- If you are a leader, what are some of the critical factors holding you or your team back that might be solved by having stronger personal brands on your team?

Now, look at the answers you have given to the questions and prioritize those challenges based on their importance to your success.

6. A strong personal brand will allow the right customers, the right employees, and the right business partners to find your company.

As mentioned before, strong personal brands become strong attractors. A strong personal brand helps you speak in shorthand to your customers, immediately drawing like-minded people to you. You want to find those customers that are seeking the experience that you and your company are offering, and a strong leadership brand helps you do that.

But your leadership brand not only calls out to your customers. It also shines out to top talent, attracting them to be "lighthouse keepers" for your company. You can find the right employees by making sure that you project your brand statement to the world in a consistent manner. People with whom your brand resonates will want to work with you and will be attracted to work with you and for you for more than just the paycheck you provide.

Having a strong leadership brand also helps you find the right business partners, like-minded individuals who want to work with you.

Actively Manage Your Personal Brand

Remember, we're looking for power and speed; that's what your branding edge will do for your career. If you are looking for a promotion within your current organization, I want you to *actively manage your personal brand* with your colleagues, your direct reports, your senior management, and colleagues in your industry. If you are a job seeker, I want you to *actively manage your personal brand* to find your way to a job that maximizes your potential, leverages your best strengths, and feeds your soul. If you are a single business practitioner, such as a real estate agent, a financial planner, or an insurance agent, I want you to *actively manage your personal brand* with your network, your clients, and potential clients. If you have been laid off, downsized, or pushed out in a restructuring, I want to make sure that you take the information in this book and say, "Never again! I'm in charge of my career, and I'm going to *actively manage my personal brand* in order to turbocharge my career!"

> *If we all did the things we are capable of doing, we would literally astound ourselves.*
> ~Thomas Edison, inventor, entrepreneur

Creating a Brand

It is a brand manager's job to create those brand interactions. If they do their jobs well, the emotional connections are forged stronger and stronger with each interaction until you would not even think of using another brand to quench your thirst or powder your baby's bottom.

I'm encouraging you to do the same thing—create interactions with your personal brand. By going through the exercises in this book, you will develop a plan that will allow you to forge the emotional connections to you and your personal brand that bring career opportunities uniquely suited to you and create your branding edge.

Are you ready to turbocharge your career? Then let's get revved up to actively manage your personal brand!

GET YOUR EDGE

To get ongoing ideas and inspiration to help you find your branding edge and turbocharge your career, sign up for regular inspiration at YourBrandingEdge.com/Newsletter.

Chapter 2

YOUR GOALS

If you don't know where you're going, any road will take you there.
—George Harrison, musician,
lead guitarist for *The Beatles*

You picked up this book to find your edge, that special something that will put you over the top—to earn that promotion, land that dream job, or work on that career-defining project. Perhaps you are looking to expand your client base, find more meaningful work, or find ways to improve your leadership skills and better manage your team. Ask yourself, "What do you want to get out of reading this book?" What effect do you expect the experience of strengthening your personal brand to have on your career?

Writing goals is very powerful. It provides structure and focus to your efforts. A few years ago, my brother reluctantly wrote out some personal goals as a part of a corporate exercise in which he was compelled to participate. The goals were in several areas of his life: finances, relationships, education, spiritual matters. He was told to be very specific about what he wanted, so he wrote as specifically as possible what his goals were. Although he was skeptical, he wrote that he wanted to transition from his current job in a distressed industry (he was working in real estate during the "mortgage meltdown") to a job that leveraged his skills more strongly and offered more stability and upward mobility; he wanted to take a trip with his son; he wanted a job where he would have more time to get involved in kids' activities; and he wanted to find ways to more strongly connect with his extended family.

He found the list again a year or so later. By that time, he was working in an opportunity-laden job in the thriving telecom industry, which was better suited for his skills. The new job also allowed him enough flexibility to coach his younger son's soccer and t-ball teams. He and his older son had also shared a once-in-a-lifetime experience in Knoxville where they got to fly a helicopter (not just fly "in" the helicopter but actually steer it!) and later that same weekend stand on the sidelines of the 104,000 capacity Neyland Stadium at a University of Tennessee football game. In addition, time had been carved out for an annual family reunion to Lake Winnipesaukee

> *The most important thing about goals is having one.*
> —Geoffrey F. Abert, author

GET YOUR EDGE

2. What are your goals?

Please answer the following questions as specifically as possible:
- What are your short-term career goals (3 months, 6 months, one year)?
- What are your long-term career goals (5 years, 10 years, 20 years)?
- If you could think really big, what would your ideal life look like five years from now?
- What does it mean to you to "turbocharge your career"?
- What are you looking for?
- What does success look like for you?

Although our focus in this book is on your professional life, feel free to think about these exercises for all aspects of your life—professional, personal, financial, social, or spiritual. Your personal brand is just that—personal; therefore, all aspects of your life will be affected by strengthening your personal brand.

Note: If you get stuck on this exercise, see the next Get Your Edge! (Assignment 3).

in New Hampshire for a week of waterskiing, playing cards, and otherwise relaxing. He discovered that every one of the goals he had written (both personal and professional) had been achieved!

Some people struggle with setting goals; however, this is a critical step in achieving your success, as it is impossible to map out a path to take you someplace if you don't know where you are going. There are several ways to approach this. Try writing down lots of goals—just keep writing until you can't think of anything else to write. Then think back on your list for a bit; those that stick in your head are probably the most meaningful to you.

GET YOUR EDGE
3. Create a vision for your future

Sometimes we are unclear about exactly what our goals are or what we might become. A simple way to draw those out is to think about the future as if it already has happened. Imagine that you are at your retirement party thinking back over your career.
- After you have retired, what do you want to have accomplished? What will your career have been about?
- What important contributions did you make?
- What was the most exciting time in your career?
- What skills did you master?
- What awards did you receive that were most meaningful to you?

Also, don't be surprised if, as you read this book, your goals shift somewhat. Sometimes what we think we want is really a shallow, "surface" type of want. As you dig deeper, you may discover more meaningful goals. At one point, I had an executive coaching assignment with a woman who wanted to be promoted either in her current job or at some other company. As we started exploring more fully why she wanted this promotion, we realized that her real need was for recognition. She wanted someone to acknowledge her contributions, and once that became apparent, a logical plan of action was easy to put in place.

GET YOUR EDGE

4. Why are these your goals?

It's important to understand why you want what you wrote down in the previous exercise. Think about the following questions:
- What do you expect to change once you achieve your goals?
- What will be different?
- What parts of this goal do you perceive are desirable and or undesirable? (that's right...even really awesome goals may have some downsides. Think that through to help you refine what you really want.)

Some people have really big dreams, and that's great. When you have a big goal, you need to make sure you are grounded in the reality of how big the goal is. If you are trying to get promoted, and thousands have gone before you and gotten promoted, that's a pretty manageable goal. But if you are trying to become the first woman president of the United States, that's a much bigger goal. I would never dissuade people from going after big goals, but I would counsel them to be realistic in the resources (time, money, working hours, and the like) needed to reach their goals.

GET YOUR EDGE

5. How big are your goals?

As you develop your goals, think about the following questions:
- Have people in your industry accomplished what you are trying to accomplish?
- How did they do it? If you can, take them to lunch to talk to them about how they did it.
- Are there any dynamics or politics you need to be mindful of?

Chapter 3

WHAT IS A PERSONAL BRAND?

What makes you unique makes you successful.
—William Arruda, motivational speaker

In order to understand personal branding, it is helpful to think about branding in general. Everyone has had experiences with brands in some way and may have some understanding of what brands are, so it's a good place to start the conversation.

Branding is my business and has been for more than twenty years. I spent my entire marketing career focused on building brands. In my personal life, I could never buy "generic" products, because it was the antithesis of what I was all about: brands. Understanding branding will lead you to understanding your personal brand.

Whenever I give talks, whether to large groups or small, to teenage students or seasoned business professionals, I always ask, "What is a brand?" Everyone has some sense of what a brand is. Some will tell you it's a product, a symbol, or a logo. Even in the marketing industry and among brand managers, people will speak of brands and logos interchangeably. While a logo acts as a visual representation of a brand, it is not the same thing as a brand. The concept of brand is much bigger than just a logo.

Often I will hear that it's an identity, something unique, something recognizable. Now we're talkin'! A brand is an idea, a concept; a brand is distinct and unique. If it's any good, a brand will create an *emotional* connection, a bond that is strong or weak, depending on the strength of the brand. It is that connection that turbocharges a product or service, and it is critical to success. It is something that people associate with a product, a service, or a company. It's the essence of that product or service that is *completely* unique to that particular experience—where nothing else is quite like it.

Brands Help Us Order Our World

A brand is an identity or image that a product, service, or company has created. It is something that uniquely identifies that product or service and differentiates it from other products in the marketplace. Because consumers have so much information thrown at them, they need a way to quickly identify a product, a service, or a company, and categorize it in their minds.

In college, I knew an exchange student who had come to America from a very small town in Brazil. She told of her first experience in an American grocery store, in particular in the cereal aisle. In her simple village store, they had a choice of three different cereals. Here in America, there are hundreds of brands of cereal featured on grocery store shelves. This woman was completely overwhelmed by the staggering array of choices on display in the cereal aisle. In fact, she walked away without choosing anything because, for her, there was too much to choose from.

This is where branding can help.

Brands help people order their world—this brand is a low-cost option, that brand is specially designed for athletes, this one is a premium product, or that one is an "everyday" kind of product. This type of reasoning and decision-making is a way of ordering a consumer's confusing world.

A brand is a differentiator, a way to distinguish your product from someone else's product. If I have a particular type of chocolate that I always buy, for example, I expect that the taste of the chocolate will always be the same (and different than anyone else's chocolate). The brand on that chocolate identifies the type of chocolate experience I am going to have, including flavor, texture, and color.

In the same way, a strong personal brand will help you stand out in a crowd—distinct among your peers and distinct among others on your leadership team. How are you differentiating yourself in your world?

GET YOUR EDGE

6. How are you differentiating yourself?

How are you different from others who do your job in other companies or industries?

A Brand is the Promise of a Future Experience

A brand creates a distinctive, ownable position in someone's mind. The objective for any brand manager is to carve out a place in someone's mind and then stay there, occupying a place in someone's thoughts and being so unique that nothing else can replace it.

If I were to ask you to choose either Wal-Mart® or Target®, Coke,® or Pepsi®, Red Sox® or Yankees®, or Nike® versus Reebok®, you could do that rather quickly, right? Depending on your mood, you'd choose easily enough. Most people don't have to struggle to think about it. They just know what they would choose.

It Works the Same for People, Too

That same principle can be applied to people. If I told you that, given a specific set of choices, you could have lunch with someone famous, whom would you choose? Will Smith, Johnny Depp, or Jim Carey? David Letterman, Conan O'Brien, or Jay Leno? Oprah or Ellen? Again, you could probably choose easily enough.

It's the same mental exercise as was done for the products. For those who know who Donald Trump is, something immediately comes to mind when they hear his name. People may love him, think he's the greatest entrepreneur, or see him as outgoing, a "take-life-by-the-horns" kind of a guy. Or they may think he is brash, outspoken, someone they would never want to be like. People may love or hate him, but he's got an extremely strong brand. He knows what he is and he communicates that very clearly.

"The Donald" is not the only one who has such a strong brand. Numerous people from all walks of life project clearly what they stand for: Oprah Winfrey, Mother Teresa, Simon Cowell, Andy Warhol, Bill Gates, Madonna, Frank Lloyd Wright, Barack Obama, Lady Gaga. What imagery comes to mind? The qualities of sacrifice and service; garish entertainment and bravado; funky, whacked-out, trail blazing; and talent all mix and mingle in that one short list of people. This is because they have built strong personal brands (even if they did so unintentionally). That's their branding edge. In the same way that brands can evoke an experience, a *person* can evoke an experience as well. All of those celebrities have very distinctive brands. These personal brands have turbocharged their careers. You know what these people stand for, you know what they are, and that is what branding and personal branding is all about.

Now you may be saying to yourself, "Come on, Oprah? She's a super-celebrity. Of course she has a brand! She's got her own magazine and her own cable channel. She's a huge, mega brand." That is true. But personal brands also exist in your everyday life, everywhere you go. Think about the person in your office who is great at problem solving. Every time you have some sticky situation that defies solution, or a particularly tangled client situation, you're going to call "Joe the Problem-Solver." Joe the Problem-Solver has found his branding edge and turbocharged his career, because when you need what he has to offer, he's the one you're going to call. Or think about the woman from the Parent-Teacher's Association. She's a master at organizing. That's what she does—she just organizes the world. She loves it and she's good at it. That's part of her personal brand. Whether she knows it or not, she has turbocharged her career.

Everyone Has a Personal Brand

Everyone has a personal brand—not just the rich and famous. Everyone in the business world can leverage their branding edge because everyone has a personal brand. If you are a leader in a company, think about those who report to you. You have very distinct ideas about your employees—"the one who can always be counted on," "the closer," "the rainmaker," "the whiner." Everyone has a distinct brand.

You, too, have a personal brand already, whether you know it or not. The type and quality of work you do is an expression of that personal brand. Tom Peters, author of the business classic *In Search of Excellence*, is considered the father of personal branding. He introduced the concept of the importance of intentionally crafting your personal brand in a *Fast*

Company article titled "The Brand Called You" and later wrote a book called *Brand You*. Peters refers to your current reputation as your "default brand." This is the brand perception that you currently convey, whether you know it or not. Peters describes it this way: "Your default brand is what people say about you when they recommend you to a client, want you on their project teams, or fix you up with their sister!" It's what you express naturally. The point of this book is to help you actively manage your personal brand—to make it as strong and compelling as possible, to help you find your branding edge.

GET YOUR EDGE

7. Personal brands in your world

Think of three people you know personally who have a strong personal brand.
- How would you describe them?
- What experience or information has led you to identify this person this way?

Be as specific as possible—a project this person did, an email he or she wrote, a story this person told, or an activity he or she participated in.

How Are Brands Created?

Brands are created by having interaction with consumers. When you go into Wal-Mart, you know what you're going to see there, and you don't expect the same experience in a Wal-Mart that you would have if you were shopping in Tiffany's®. That's because they are very different brands. You have certain expectations of both, and you expect that each time you go to Wal-Mart it's going to be the same experience. You may love Wal-Mart. You may say, "I can get anything I want; it's a brilliant place. The prices are so low; it's just wonderful." Or you may say, "I hate Wal-Mart. It's dirty and jumbled, and what is up with that greeter at the front of the store?" Whatever it is, that's part of the brand for you.

The choice of which brand to use becomes easier the more interaction you have with a particular brand. Why? Because those experiences are carving out a place in your mind, either good or bad. There's a shared

GET YOUR EDGE

8. What is your current reputation?

Tom Peters describes your default brand as "what people say about you when they recommend you to a client, want you on their project teams, or fix you up with their sister!"
- Write down what you think your "default" brand is. Remember to include both positive and negative aspects of that brand.
- What actions, activities, or events have caused that perception?

history that gets built up, based on interactions with the brand. You gain experience with it, and that makes you say, "Yes I relate to that; I like that brand," or "I don't like that brand."

Usually, those interactions are very deliberate. Brand managers are paid to develop marketing plans full of consumer interactions, such as television commercials, public relations stories pitched to the newspaper, movie product placements, package design enhancements, or sampling programs.

But sometimes the interaction is quite accidental. For example, at a party someone is overheard talking about a terrible experience they had with a lawn service company, or perhaps a friend at the party offers you a type of soft drink you normally do not drink. In either case, you have gained exposure, and you have gained an experience with that brand. That experience combines with everything else you know about that brand to create an image in your mind about that brand's promise.

That's why a brand is so much more than a logo. Yes, a visual can connote a brand, and that is part of it. But it is all those experiences consumers have with a product or service that put meaning into the visual.

When you add up all the different experiences you have with a specific brand (whether it is a product or a person), you have developed a shared history with that brand, and there is an expectation that the brand will provide that experience every time. The same happens with others' experience with you as a brand. For example, if you are a creative person, then people will expect you to be creative again. If you are always prompt, people will expect that you will not be late.

GET YOUR EDGE

9. What are some of your favorite brands?

Think of some really strong brands with which you have a strong emotional connection.
- What experiences have built the passion for that brand in your mind and heart?
- What has this brand done to create such a compelling connection for you?
- How can you relate that to your personal brand?

Chapter 4

BE CLEAR

> Today you are YOU!
> That is truer than true!
> There is no one alive
> That is You-er than YOU!
>
> —Dr. Seuss

Expressing your personal brand should be as easy as breathing. It's who you are and what you are all about. But what I'm talking about here is *actively managing* your personal brand, and that takes a bit more effort. Building an expertise in branding takes years, whether you're talking about branding a bucket of bricks, a box of plant food, or you. But my goal is to teach you shortcuts to help you crystallize what you are all about and clearly communicate that personal brand to the people in your world in a high-impact way that is authentic to who you are. This is your branding edge.

I've boiled it down to seven main strategies for personal branding success, and we will go through them one by one. Each one is important, and they are all interrelated, building one upon another.

Remember, you are the brand manager in charge of your brand. In order to turbocharge your career, you must take an active role in this. In my coaching programs, I work with individuals over the course of months to bring clarity to their brands and put an action plan in place for clearly expressing those brands. Each of these principles starts with the verb "be." That is very deliberate; I did that on purpose. While you naturally express your personal brand (it is a naturally state of "be-ing"), you need to be a *participant* here—you need to *do* something. These concepts will not benefit you unless you actively manage your personal brand. This book will guide you to do just that.

GET YOUR EDGE

Seven Principles of Personal Branding

> You can download the seven principles as a one-page summary to help you remember these critical branding strategies at YourBrandingEdge.com/BookExtras.

Be Clear

To build your personal brand, you need to be clear about who you are and what you have to offer. We're looking for clarity about what is unique about you and what is core to your brand. This is the first of the seven principles. Who are you? What are you all about? In order for us to build an action plan for clearly expressing your brand, we have to know what it is we want to express. Makes sense, right?

Brand managers take time to get clear in their minds about what critical qualities they want to be expressed. They ask pointed questions: "What does my brand stand for, and what do I want my consumers to think about my brand?" "What qualities do I want them to associate with my brand?" And in the case of a new product introduction or extension, "What new qualities of my brand do I need to convey?"

You Are Unique

In the beginning of this book, I told you that you are unique. You are one of a kind. Take the quality of "funny." Everyone reading this book has a sense of humor in varying degrees. You might have a very dry sense of humor, while someone else has a more "slapstick" sense of humor. Your personal brand is defined in part by how you express the quality of humor, and the world needs all of these various degrees of that quality.

Think about comedians like Bill Cosby, Ellen Degeneres, Jim Carey, Chris Rock, Dane Cook, and Jerry Seinfeld. Each uses different kinds of humor. Is there only demand for one comedian in the world? Of course not. We love them all! There's a whole comedy channel dedicated to showcasing different types of comedians. Not all comedians will appeal to everyone, but there is value in each comedian's unique perspective on our world.

And that's an example of just one quality! Multiply that by all the other distinct qualities you have, and you can see how you are truly unique.

You want to be very clear about who you are because of this uniqueness. It's personal to you; it's *your* branding edge. It's like a signature, and everyone's signature is a little bit different. It's imperative that you understand your uniqueness so you can convey it to others clearly.

When you're in middle school, you just want to fit in. Standing out, being different, being one-of-a-kind can be uncomfortable for young people who are just beginning to understand who they are and can cause social awkwardness. But for marketers, being unique is what it's all about, because no one wants to buy what they perceive as "me-too" products. People seek out something special, something one-of-a-kind. The same applies to people. Those who are different, unique, and one of a kind tend to stand out in a crowd and find it easier to "make a name for themselves." Actors who can find their own style have more earning potential and can end up with roles that advance their careers in exciting and dynamic ways. They have effectively "turbocharged their careers." Some examples include Meryl Streep, Jack Nicholson, Katherine Hepburn, Dustin Hoffman, and Tom Hanks.

When you are talking about personal branding and its impact on your career, you absolutely want to be different. Brand managers work very hard and spend tens of thousands of dollars to understand the nuances of their brands versus the competition so they can highlight those differences in their marketing efforts. That's what you want to do, too—understand your personal brand. Find out how you are different and then celebrate that. Shout it out to the world, and make people see how different you are and what great contributions you have to offer.

What Are You Good At?

During a corporate training session at a major toy company, I asked a group of professionals to write down twenty qualities about themselves or twenty strengths of their personal brand. One woman looked completely dumbfounded. She stared down at the blank sheet of paper and finally said,

GET YOUR EDGE

10. Who do you think you are? (Part I)

> Take some time to write down at least three of your qualities or skills in each of the following areas:
> - **Skills:** These are usually specific job-related skills, the "what" of your job (forecasting, analysis, planning).
> - **Hobbies/talents:** These are your professional and personal passions or gifts that you have to share with the world, which are also reflected in your personal world (horseback riding, creative writing, organization).
> - **Attributes:** This is the "how" of what you do and is usually more attitudinal (cheerful, creative, funny).
>
> You should have at least nine qualities, skills, and attributes on your list. As you move forward, you will hone in on the ones you think are most core to who you are. Future exercises in this book will use what you identify in this exercise.
>
> As you identify these qualities and skills, think about how each gets expressed in your life. If you are creative, do you wear colorful clothes? If you are organized, do you have a super-neat desk? Write down how someone would know that these skills and attributes are a part of your brand. To help you in this exercise, you can download a list of qualities from YourBrandingEdge.com/BookExtras.

"Rahna, that's got to be the hardest thing you could've asked for!" She was stumped. She had no idea what to write and, sadder still, she had no idea what she was good at! This is a woman in a very well-known company that conducts annual formal performance reviews, and *still* she didn't know.

Unfortunately, I see this all too often. People have no idea what value they bring to their world, what strengths they have, what qualities they have to contribute.

This is a crime. This is why I do what I do. All people need to know what they are good at. If people understood their own strengths more clearly, they would have more self-esteem and they would seek out opportunities to maximize those talents, and *rock their world!*

GET YOUR EDGE

List of Qualities

In one session I conducted, someone asked for a list of qualities to choose from, as she lamented that she could not think of any qualities on her own. If you are struggling with coming up with qualities, here's a partial list of qualities to choose from:

Approachable	Efficient	Inspiring	Persistent
Calm	Empowering	Joyful	Problem-solver
Caring	Fun	Kind	Self-aware
Competent	Funny	Knowledgeable	Smart
Confident	Hard-working	Organized	Steadfast
Creative	High energy	Passionate	Tenacious

You can download a more complete list of hundreds of qualities at YourBrandingEdge.com/BookExtras.

GET YOUR EDGE

11. Who do you think you are? (Part II)

Building on the previous assignment, answer the following questions:
- How would you describe yourself?
- What are you really good at?
- What do you like about yourself?
- What don't you like about yourself?
- What is your current work style?
- What is your place within the company? Think in terms of budgetary responsibility, percentage of total employee base managed, percentage of total sales volume generated/managed.

If it's not an easy exercise for you, even that fact is an indicator that you need to really focus on this. But don't be alarmed. Simply take the time now to identify what is great about you. Self-awareness is a critical part of strong personal branding.

If you don't know what your talents are, *go find out!*

One of the assignments calls for you to ask several of your business colleagues, your girlfriends, your spouse, your golfing buddies, or family members to tell you at least four things they appreciate about you. You want to ask a cross-section of people from the different areas of your life so you can get a well-rounded picture of what's great about you.

> *Getting in touch with your true self must be your first priority.*
> —Tom Hopkins, author, sales trainer, speaker

Ask for qualities they feel you express, and seek to understand why that adds value to their lives. What is it about you that is so great? Why are you so important in their lives? What value do you bring to them? Why do they seek you out? And be sure to ask for both the positive and the negative.

My husband will tell you that I don't really have a great sense of time. I get lost in my work, and I'm always late. But he also knows that I'm passionate, that I'm creative, that I love my work, and that I have high energy and enthusiasm for life. These are things that are all part of my brand. You want to understand all the different aspects of your brand.

Try to be as specific as possible. You want to understand the nuances of these qualities in order to understand what makes you unique. You want to understand the subtleties about your strengths and how you are different from everyone else.

So please, if you care about advancing your career in amazing ways, find out about what Tom Peters referred to as your "default" brand. It is a foundational piece of information for radical career growth both inside a corporate environment and on your own. Understanding your unique value helps you "sell" yourself to others. And make no mistake about it: In your career, you are *always* selling yourself.

If you were in the Indy pit crew, you would need to understand all the nuances of your car's engine in order to squeeze maximum performance out of it. The same applies to your personal brand. You must understand the nuances of your brand in order to turbocharge your career.

I can guarantee that as you hear back from those friends, neighbors, co-workers, and family members, a few key qualities will bubble up. You will hear the same types of comments over and over again—because we are who we are, whether we are at home or at work. We may have slightly different aspects of those qualities show up more in one environment than in another, but those core strengths will show themselves in many areas of your life.

GET YOUR EDGE

12. Who do others think you are?

Ask three or four people to answer the following questions. Encourage these people to be honest in their feedback. This is important learning, as it will allow you to see yourself as others currently see you. In addition, please answer these questions for yourself.
The people you ask should be from several different areas of your life, including:
- Workplace connections (colleagues, employees, senior management, clients)
- Family
- Friends
- Community (religious, civic, political, leisure activities)

Ask them these questions:
1. How would you describe me?
2. What would you say are my greatest talents?
3. What areas would you like to see me grow in?

What Is Your Backstory?

To further clarify your brand, it can be helpful to identify past influences in your life. How did your brand develop into what you are today? Where did your brand come from?

Every brand has a story. It doesn't matter whether it's the story of how Coke was started in the 1800's or how Spotify launched as a start-up in 2008, there is heritage that goes along with every brand. The roots of a brand can affect and build that brand. Brand managers and public relations specialists understand that it is helpful to manage the heritage story. Many brands have a strong story that goes along with what they are all about. Hewlett-Packard got started from two guys putting together a computer in a garage. Bill Gates quit Harvard in order to start Microsoft. Brands have stories that go along with them, and people love to tell those stories. That's a big part of branding.

The same principle can apply to you as well. What's your story? Trace your passions back because understanding your story will help you convey to others why you are who you are. For example, my backstory is that I spent many years in corporate marketing departments, building some of America's strongest brands, like LEGO toys, Miracle-Gro plant food, Build-A-Bear Workshop, and Texaco gasoline. When I went out on my own, I had to really analyze what my core strengths were in order to convey why someone should hire me. I did exactly what I am telling you to do in this book. I soon realized that all those brand-building skills could be applied to people, too, and that was much more rewarding to me. That's how I got interested in personal branding. That was the genesis of this book and of my adding "personal branding strategist" to my personal brand.

GET YOUR EDGE

13. What's your backstory?

Think about why you are the way you are. Can you find clues to your inquisitive nature in your childhood? Have you always been a tinkerer, a dreamer, a reader, an animal lover? Write out some of the major aspects of your back story.

What Do You Want to Be?

So far, we've talked about who you are and what qualities you currently express, and that's critical to understand. But a good personal brand manager will take that to the next level, to ask that next question: "What do you *want* to be?" The answer to this question is critical and should tie directly to the goals you established in the Goals chapter.

Maybe there are some qualities that you would like to possess but that you don't currently have. Perhaps some qualities are part of your personal brand that you wish weren't. As they relate to your career, explore those qualities that are highly valued in your industry. Think about the people in your industry who have had a meteoric rise in the company or someone you admire, someone you respect a great deal. What qualities does that person express? What qualities and skills are critical to success in your industry?

GET YOUR EDGE

14. Whom do you admire?

> Write down the names of three people you admire and why you admire them. What qualities do they have that you admire?

These are things you might want to consider adding to your skill set. Don't worry if you don't have these qualities now because we will map out *how* to add new skills. Right now I simply want you to capture the thoughts that come to you. Anyone can add skills if they choose to, and we'll talk more about that in Chapter 10.

Adding to Your Personal Brand

The qualities you admire that are not a part of your personal brand right now could be in the future. In his book *Outliers*, Malcolm Gladwell puts forth the idea that if you want to be a world-class expert like the Beatles or Bill Gates, it takes 10,000 hours to do so. That translates to approximately ten years at three and a half to four hours per day, five days a week. If you're already working in that discipline, it would take about five years to become an expert. While that is a lot of time, it is not an impossible amount of time. It doesn't matter how old or young you are now, you should take the time to continually add to your personal brand. If you're 40 right now, and you live to be 80, you've got as much time ahead of you as you've got behind you. That's a long time to develop a lot of great skills. If you're 20, just think of all the qualities you can add to your personal brand over time! Even if you're in your 60s and live to be 80, that is 20 years to build your personal brand. That's an entire career to build and grow and *do*.

You can develop into whatever you want. So what do you want to be known for? Think about that and go get it. Add that quality to your personal brand.

What Do You Want to Be Known For?

What do you want to be known for? If you don't want to be the spreadsheet guru, what do you want to be? There should be no limits at this point. Think big. Dream. *Really* think about who you are and what you would like to be. Maybe you want to write a book. Maybe you want to climb Mount Everest. Whatever you want to do, write that down as something you want to be known for.

You Can Create Any Personal Brand You Want

Many people think they have no control over the way they are. They say, "That's just who I am" or "My past has made me the way I am" or "My circumstances have made me who I am." And while it's true those things may have influenced you or may have shaped you in the past, that sort of mindset is not productive—and not true. You are in complete control of your brand. While it may have influenced the development of your current personal brand, your past doesn't have to dictate your future. We're talking about activating and maximizing your potential. Potential is a current and future activity. If you really want to turbocharge your career, you must develop the mindset that you have control over what you are and what you become.

> *God didn't have time to make a nobody, only a somebody. I believe that each of us has God-given talents within us waiting to be brought to fruition.*
> —Mary Kay Ash, entrepreneur and founder of Mary Kay Cosmetics

In college, I was an art history major. Actually, I was a double major in English and art history, which is not so helpful on a resume, as it is not very business-oriented. I did minor in business, but that's not the same. Yet I always knew that I wanted to go into marketing and business.

When I graduated from college, I knew exactly what I wanted to do, and I kept at it until I got the job I wanted. I convinced one of the top New York ad agencies that I was just what they needed. I was determined and persistent —those are two of the qualities of my personal brand. I got a job in one of the last remaining account executive training programs in the Big Apple. But I always felt as though I was behind everyone else. I felt that because I was not a business major or an MBA out of Wharton, I wasn't as good as others. I was sure there was something they knew that I didn't know. I felt like I needed more work, specifically in the area of numbers—in quantitative skills. I knew that I wanted eventually to be a brand manager, and that I would need to be able to look at a balance sheet and really talk with the financial folks in the company.

So I did something about it. Every time there was any kind of analysis work, I offered to do that work so that I could research numbers, understand spreadsheets and see how "cost of goods" worked. I did all kinds of analyses and became really comfortable with numbers. Throughout my corporate career, I have managed annual budgets as large as $72 million. And in one of my last reviews before I left The LEGO Group, my boss said, "You have great strength in forecasting."

My college friends would have fallen off their chairs laughing about that. But I had taken the time to learn those financial skills because I wanted to be good with numbers. That doesn't mean I was ever going to become an accountant, but at least I'd developed a competency with numbers.

That's what you may need to do. Decide what you would like to add to the list of qualities you currently have. Then, in your action planning, think about how you might go about adding whatever quality you want.

I have been talking about the power of personal branding throughout this most recent recession, and, while there are many who have heart-wrenching stories to tell, others have been energized by the thought of reinventing themselves, daring to dream and explore what they could be. You need to have that same spirit of change, even if you have been in an incredibly stable corporate job for years. Whether we are aware of it or not, we reinvent ourselves daily. Make sure the new you is better than who you were yesterday.

GET YOUR EDGE

15. What skills do you want to add to your personal brand?

Answer the following questions:
- What skills are valued in your industry?
- What other skills would you like to add to your personal brand?

Eliminating Qualities from Your Personal Brand

In the list that comes back from your friends or colleagues, there may be some things you don't like. There are always going to be some negative aspects of your personal brand that you'll want to work on improving over time. But don't despair. You can always change. Think about what you were like ten years ago, even five years ago. Are you the same now as you were then? Absolutely not. You may be very similar, but the experiences of your life have changed you. Progress is a natural part of our being, and it is absolutely a part of actively managing your personal brand.

Rebranding Yourself

One question I'm asked a lot when I speak about this topic is, "What if there is something that is part of my personal brand that I don't want to be anymore?" Because we are ever growing, we sometimes "outgrow" aspects of our personal brand that once were perhaps core to who we were, but that we no longer want to be known for. Often, people feel "pigeonholed" into being only one thing.

> *Change is never a matter of ability; it is always a matter of motivation.*
> —Tony Robbins, Motivational speaker, author, coach

The solution is to add other qualities and put the focus on those areas that you see as part of your future, not as part of your past. Actors have to deal with this quite often. As actors manage their careers, they will actively seek out roles that are different from

GET YOUR EDGE

16. What do you want to eliminate from your personal brand?

Answer the following questions:
- What don't you like about yourself?
- What would you like to eliminate from your personal brand?
- What parts of your job don't you like?

So, what qualities would you like to eliminate? Are you a procrastinator? Maybe you're shy. Maybe you're scatterbrained. This is very personal work, so dig deep!

roles they have played in the past in order to avoid being "typecast" as one particular type of character. Actors who allow themselves to get into such a rut can quickly become bored, so they make specific efforts to avoid this. A classic example is Tom Hanks' career. He started as a comedic actor with a lead role in *Bosom Buddies*, *Joe Versus the Volcano*, and *Bachelor Party*. He made specific strides in stretching his personal brand with very serious roles in *Philadelphia* and then *Forest Gump*.

Now think about your own career. Are you bored with the projects you are being given? Would you like to stretch your wings and try something new? Become known for more than you currently are? All of this is possible if you set a purposeful plan to become more than you are today. You do not have to be limited by what you are today. Build a bridge from today to become what you would like to be tomorrow.

Christine's Story—Be Clear

As owner of Stitch Design Studio in Pomfret Center, Connecticut, Christine Kalafus was principal designer of the elegant window treatments and other furnishings she created for her clients.

Christine was laser-focused on developing, refining, and expressing her brand and that activity transformed her career. She paid her way through college as a licensed insurance agent and earned a bachelor's degree in interior design from the University of New Haven. She was successful in the insurance industry, which made it hard to quit. Sometimes, excellent pay and benefits can cause inertia that can keep us from fully expressing our personal brand. But a life-changing victory over cancer made her realize that life is too short to settle for a career she didn't love. Nine years after college, by then married and the mother of three children, she finally made the leap to pursue her passion.

She had sewn her whole life, but she knew she had to take her skills to the next level. For three years, she apprenticed for a woman who is "a genius at engineering fabric." From this woman, she learned master craftsman skills that became a signature for her success. When she decided to start her own business, she signed up for a class at the University of Hartford's Entrepreneurial Center. That's where she met me; I taught there as adjunct professor of branding and marketing for several years.

Christine reported, "That's where I learned about focusing on one thing; you can't be diverse. You have to understand what your specialty is because that is what is going to carry you." Through her experiences in insurance and her personal life, she gained clarity about her goals, her strengths, and her desires. She then actively pursued those passions.

You Can't Get Rid of a Negative; You Can Only Add a Positive

A vital part of gaining clarity about your personal brand includes determining what changes you would like to make. When I am coaching people on this, I advise them that they cannot eliminate a negative; they can only add a positive. When you are thinking about this in relation to your own personal brand, you need to think in terms of adding some positive quality that will naturally eliminate an undesirable negative quality.

Remember how I said that my husband doesn't think I'm very good with time? That would be a negative on my list: always late. That might be something I would choose to work on, to eliminate, to take off the list.

But I cannot *not* be late. I have to *add* "timeliness" to my personal brand.

How would I do this? Well, I would put together a plan to help me get better at this—maybe I set my watch five minutes fast. Maybe I hang huge clocks in my office, in my kitchen, around my house to help me improve my time management. There's an old saying that whatever you focus on expands. I have found that to be true, so if you focus on adding a new desirable quality to your personal brand, you are bound to improve.

GET YOUR EDGE

17. What do you want to eliminate from your personal brand?

Thinking about the negatives, take some time to identify the opposites (or positives) you would like to add to your personal brand. How might you go about this?

What Is Your Leadership Brand?

Many people fall (or are thrust) into leadership positions by their extreme competence in a given area, but they don't give much thought to what type of leader they want to be. If you are leading a team or a project, you need to consider the perceptions of others as they relate to your leadership brand. In our corporate workshops and coaching programs, we challenge leaders to think about the specific messages they convey to their direct reports, their broader teams, and their senior management and colleagues. These sessions are very personal, as most leaders discover they are passionate about something—customer service, absolute quality, excellence in their field, never giving up. Identifying this aspect of your brand will help as you develop an action plan for how to convey this leadership to interested parties.

GET YOUR EDGE

18. What is your leadership brand?

Answer the following questions:
- What do you stand for?
- How can you best contribute to your team, your company, and your community?
- What specific action plans are you executing to project your leadership brand to others?
- Do you have actionable plans in place to increase your exposure to either internal or external target audiences to increase your influence to your colleagues, your clients, and your world?
- What is your personal leadership brand?

Determining the brand of a person is a lot more difficult than determining the brand of a product or service, because people are so much more complicated than a can of Coke. Your light is at the same time ever constant and ever changing—ever constant because it's been with you since you were born and ever changing because you are constantly evolving. So be patient with yourself as you go through this process.

Being clear about who you are and what wonderful things you have to offer is the foundation for all the other principles presented later in this book. It's a lot of thought work. Clarifying your branding edge is the work of a lifetime, but it is well worth the effort.

Once you have thought all this through, you can determine what your personal brand is, and what you would like it to be. Then, you can put a plan in place to express and improve your personal brand.

Chapter 5

BE CONFIDENT

Without a humble but reasonable confidence in your own powers, you cannot be successful or happy.

—Norman Vincent Peale, author and motivational speaker

When Mario Andretti stomps his foot down on the accelerator to demand performance from his racecar, he expects the turbochargers to kick into action. He has confidence that they will get him what he needs. You must have the same confidence in your personal brand to turbocharge your career.

Be confident! This strategy is the most critical of all those we will discuss. Let me say that again: This strategy is the most critical of all those we will discuss. You must believe in yourself. Of all the principles we talk about in this book and in our programs, this is the one that trips most people up. I want to make sure that you grasp the concepts in this chapter so you can maximize your potential to your world.

Positively Projecting Your Value

When it comes down to it, your branding edge is about positively projecting your unique value to those who matter to you, whether they are your clients, your colleagues, or your loved ones. It is a form of sales; you are selling yourself. If you were to ask the highest-paid sales strategists like Brian Tracy, they would tell you how important confidence is in the selling process. It's the No. 1 quality of a great salesperson. It doesn't matter whether they're smooth talkers; it's not that they know the product line the best. It's not about whether they went to Harvard or Stanford. It's foundationally whether they have high self-esteem. If you want to build a highly functioning sales team, you need people who have a sense of their worth, a sense of the value they can bring to their clients. And if you want to have a strong personal brand, then you need confidence. You need to cultivate high self-esteem, especially in professional settings.

So many people have been laid off, downsized, right-sized, or otherwise "made redundant" (ugh, I hate that phrase), and it has rocked people's sense of self-worth. But you *must* express confidence. If you were looking for a job, you wouldn't go in to an interview with your head down, dragging your feet, and say in a mousy voice, "Here's my resume. You wouldn't want to hire me, would you?" No! A confident person would be prepared, would have looked at the challenges the company faces and would say with confidence, "You know, I've studied your company and your markets. You are doing a great job in these five areas, but boy, in this other area, I'd love to find out what you are doing. I really think that I can add something because I see opportunities for you here, here, and here."

Which candidate would you want to hire? Of course you would choose the one who had the confidence! So if you want to express your personal brand in a strong way, then you need to have confidence.

On reality talent shows like *American Idol*® or *America's Got Talent*®, the people who do well are those who "own the stage." It doesn't necessarily have to be expressed as bravado, although bravado certainly helped Fantasia Barrino win the third season of *American Idol*. It can simply be a quiet confidence that is born of an understanding that you have something unique to bring to your world. How can you "own" your stage?

> *My lips are big, but my talent is bigger.*
> —Fantasia Barrino, American Idol winner, third season

You Are Not Commonplace

Earlier, we discussed the fact that you are unique, that you are one of a kind, and that you need to have extreme clarity about that uniqueness. You also need to know that you are worthy.

Everyone has inherent value, and you need to respect that. No one else can do things the way you do. And you need to know that—I mean at a gut level, *know it*. That is very hard for a lot of people. Our whole lives we've been told, "Don't brag." But you must have confidence in order to have a strong personal brand.

The Difference Between Self-Confidence and Self-Centeredness

Confidence in yourself wells up within you when you explore and see the value you can create for the world. Confidence is a belief in oneself and one's abilities to contribute, whereas self-centeredness puts self before all else. One is inwardly focused; the other is focused on others. I am not advocating that you become an arrogant, selfish, self-centered person. I am simply telling you that in order to successfully manage your personal brand and grow and develop in your career, you need to have a healthy dose of self-worth. That sense of self-worth will convey itself to the world around you. The process of actively managing your personal brand is helping the world see a positive and authentic image of you.

Expressing Our Personal Brand Is as Easy as Breathing

It's so very easy to undervalue ourselves. We tend to think the qualities we express are commonplace, because we live with ourselves every day. The core qualities of our personal brand come as easily to us as breathing. We don't have to think about them. We simply and naturally express them. Carrie Underwood was singing to the cows for years before she stepped in front of the judges of *American Idol*. To Carrie, her voice is "normal." Of course, to the rest of us, her voice is amazing.

The same holds true for you. To others, your particular skills and qualities are not commonplace, and they do not come easily. That's one of the wonderful aspects of this wide world of ours, that everyone has unique talents to contribute and we all contribute those in our own way. Holly has been my virtual assistant for the past several years, and she is (of course) ultra-organized. She doesn't have to actively think about expressing order; she *simply is* organized. It's part of her personal brand. And it's a major benefit to me! That's why I pay her.

Naturally, Holly thinks everyone thinks the way that she does. But that's not true. And that's a critical aspect of understanding her value. You need to find those things that you do easily, as easily as breathing. They are the clues to understanding your personal brand.

I am organized chaos. Everything is out on my desk. I can usually find whatever I need, but it's not the picture-perfect personification of orderliness. But I love to give talks, to inspire a roomful of people to realize the power of their personal brand. My passion for this topic is definitely a part of my personal brand, and that is my value.

So what is it you do that is so great? Find your value, understand your worth, and express your personal brand with confidence!

Some have a very difficult time with this. They say, "How can I have confidence in myself? I just got laid off, and I feel useless." Certainly, there are events in our lives that make us feel like we just got kicked in the teeth—getting fired, being served divorce papers, losing the business pitch to your biggest competitor (again!). I completely understand that. But the way out of that lack of self-worth is to figure out what your personal brand is and then express it!

Confidence-Building Signature Stories

Often, we need to be reminded of the good we have done, building upon the past in order to express confidence for the future. One great way to build this confidence is to write down not only the strengths and accomplishments you've expressed throughout your career, but also to recap specific times when you expressed that particular quality or skill. This is also helpful when you need to articulate your personal brand to others in a non-offensive, non-bragging manner; we'll be talking more about that when we discuss how to be bold.

I call these your "signature stories." These are short summaries that give concrete examples of how and when you expressed a quality. In order to break it down and make it somewhat more manageable, you can think in terms of a formula that might be helpful in the development of your signature stories. First, briefly explain the situation. Then you want to highlight the opportunity that existed or the challenge to be overcome. Tell what you did to resolve the issue, and end with the results that came of your actions. Here's an example:

As you can imagine, working in the marketing department on LEGO toy campaigns required a certain amount of creativity and a sense of innovation in my daily job. At one point, I had to get the word out about a new product line called Exo-Force. This was a product line of LEGO sets built around the premise that humans and robots were battling for ultimate control of the world. With a limited advertising budget, I had to build exposure for the product line, so I worked with a team to develop an animated story that brought the battle to life for boys. Using both on-air and online components, we partnered with Nickelodeon® to reveal parts of the story over an extended period of time. Shepherding this program through execution required a lot of persistence, patience, and tactful communication with multiple parties, as neither the internal team nor Nickelodeon had done something like this before. Boys loved it! The program built interest and enthusiasm for the line and drew traffic to the website. That year, it became one of the biggest product lines within its category and earned the company millions of dollars in revenue.

There. I just told you a signature story. In less than one minute, I was able to give you an example of some skills and qualities that are part of my personal brand (creativity, innovation, persistence, patience, communication skills). The formula goes like this:

Skill: Innovation

Situation: Introducing LEGO Exo-Force

Challenge: Build exposure on limited budget

Action: Develop animation and divide it up over time; work with team to shepherd through Nickelodeon's approval processes

Results: Millions of dollars in sales for the company

Completing this exercise will help build your confidence. It's important for you to outline specific times when you have expressed various qualities or skills. Once you start to think of examples, you'll be able to see how you have expressed those qualities. When you are feeling vulnerable, you can come back to these stories to bolster your confidence and move forward.

GET YOUR EDGE

19. Exemplify your strengths and skills

Build a file of your signature stories. Continue to build these stories over time, adding to your storehouse of successes to build your confidence.

Strengths

List your key strengths on separate pieces of paper (or index cards). Underneath each strength, provide an example of that strength in action. Briefly describe the situation, the barriers you had to overcome or the opportunity that existed, what actions you took, and the results.

Accomplishments

Some people have an easier time focusing on their accomplishments. Think of a major project you were involved with and build a signature story for that. List the accomplishment, then briefly describe the situation, the barriers you had to overcome, what actions you took, and the results achieved.

If you'd like a guideline for this exercise, visit YourBrandingEdge.com/BookExtras for a downloadable signature stories form.

If you cannot think of a story for a particular quality or skill, ask others for help. If it is truly a part of your personal brand, then a signature story exists. It simply needs to be brought out.

If you don't have any stories for a particular skill, then it isn't (yet) a part of your personal brand. In that case, part of your action plan would be to look for and create opportunities to build signature stories around that desirable quality or skill.

Know Your Value

Building your confidence is critical to success. I know from firsthand experience. I have applied these principles to myself as well—in fact, I am the No. 1 "test case" for all the concepts discussed in this book. When I decided to step out of the corporate world and go into business for myself, I had to determine my brand and my value proposition. I got some great advice when I was working through this challenging question: "What is it I have to bring? There are millions of marketers out there; how am I different?" Someone recommended that I write down five things I did well every day. Over a whole year, that translates to more than a thousand things that I did well. This exercise is not meant to have me brag or say, "Well, I'm better than everyone else in the world." It's meant to show me that I have value.

> *No one can figure out your worth but you.*
> —Pearl Bailey, Tony-award winning actress and singer

Some days, that value was shown to a pretty small audience, by making a peanut butter and jelly sandwich for my daughter. Other days, I would give a talk to a roomful of corporate professionals, and my value would be shown there. But each, as it turns out, is an audience of inestimable value to me. In both instances, I brought value to someone's world.

You may be saying to yourself, "But I'm not the head of a major division of a Fortune 500 company." So many people feel they are "only a lowly manager" or "only a part-time teacher" or "useless because I'm out of a job." You cannot afford that kind of thinking—not if you are building a strong personal brand! You must honor the value you bring, even if it is only to one client or one person that you are supporting.

GET YOUR EDGE

Journal Resource

If you need to build your self-esteem, I recommend writing down five things every day that you did well. If you'd like a guideline for daily journaling, visit YourBrandingEdge.com/BookExtras for a downloadable daily form.

Confidence Is Not Comparative

Having confidence is not comparative. It is not a question of being better than the next guy. It's simply about you understanding that you have value. Because each of you can write down five things you've done well each day for a year, and you, too, will have more than a thousand things on your list. And that's the beautiful thing. Everyone who is reading this book has value; you are magnificent and have unique skills, talents, and perspectives to bring to your world.

Maybe you have a lot of baggage. Maybe the list of the qualities you don't want to be known for is longer than the list of your current strengths. Don't worry. Even a heavily loaded plane can take off. All it has to do is to start moving forward. Just start. Just try. Just do something. And you will begin to understand what is unique about you, and you will start to express more and more of that personal brand in stronger and stronger ways.

> *Even a heavily loaded plane can take off. All it has to do is to start moving forward.*

It's Hard to Be Confident When You're Evolving

When we are trying to grow, it's hard to be confident, especially when we are just learning a new skill. When I volunteered for projects that required financial analysis, I was very much an art history major, which is to say, I wasn't very good at it. It certainly didn't feel like I was "breathing." But I practiced, and now I'm very comfortable with financials. It doesn't mean I'm going to become a Certified Public Accountant, but I am comfortable talking about financials with my clients. I can look at their budgets, ask about cost of goods, profit and loss, and all those sorts of numeric topics. I built up a competence (and my confidence along with that) over time. And you can do the same.

We'll talk more in the next chapter about being prepared, but just know that practice and preparedness will also help you increase your confidence. If you have done something a million times before, you can have confidence that you will be able to do it again.

While you may not have much confidence in whatever the skill is that you are working to master, you can have confidence in your ability to grow and evolve and learn. At one point in your life, you did not know how to walk or talk or multiply. Each of those skills was mastered (usually with a lot of falling down involved); have confidence that you can master new skills, too.

> ### Christine's Story — Be Confident
>
> In any career change, especially a massive reinvention such as Christine's, fears and doubts need to be overcome. "Am I too old?" "Did I miss out?" "Is it too late?" "Am I under-qualified?" "Is it worth the effort?" These questions plagued her and they may plague you. As she progressed, Christine's thinking shifted from "Can I really do this?" to "What can't I do? There are endless possibilities!"
>
> Buoyed by her husband's support, she burned her insurance license in the kitchen one evening—a terrifying yet empowering act that forced her to find who she was and what she wanted to become. She started working out of her home office and networking with others. Soon, word quickly spread about her upscale designs and accessible nature. She established her practice client by client, gaining confidence with each one. "There's definitely a learning curve, but I developed unique techniques that thrilled my clients. My business began to grow."
>
> It doesn't make a difference at what level your business is; confidence is something you may always wrestle with. The president of a company has doubts and fears about his or her capabilities just as much as the college student right out of graduate school. The key is to keep on expressing your brand in your authentic way.
>
> When an opportunity came along for a fabulously inexpensive retail space, she had doubts again about taking her business to that next level. But she made the space her own, immediately putting fresh flowers out front and making sure her sign was just the way she wanted it to be, and her business flourished.

Be Careful How You Talk to Yourself

Another thing you can do to build your self-confidence is to eliminate self-condemnation. It doesn't do you any good to beat yourself up over things you've done or things that have happened to you. It is so important that you have high self-esteem and if you're continually beating yourself up about whatever has gone wrong, you'll never get there. Lou Holtz, former football coach of Notre Dame and South Carolina, once admonished that God gave us two eyes in the front of our heads so that we could see the future and told us that we should not waste time worrying about the past. I pass that bit of wisdom on to you. Don't focus on what was. Focus on what is going to be. Be confident that you *can* improve, that you *can* learn this skill, that you *can* win that client over—because with that kind of attitude, you're going to build a very strong personal brand.

> *Think twice before you speak, because your words and influence will plant the seed of either success or failure in the mind of another.*
> —Napoleon Hill, author

How you talk to yourself is incredibly important. Don't allow negative thoughts to convince you that you don't measure up, that you're not worthy, because the truth of the matter is that you have unique skills to bring to the world and nobody can do things the way you do.

Be Careful How Others Talk to You

We'll talk more about networking in a later chapter, but the people you choose to hang out with can have an impact on your personal brand as well. You want to be around people who are on your side, people who build you up, increase your skill set, and add to your talent. Make sure you choose the people you hang out with carefully so they add to your confidence.

Do not listen to others' condemnation. Don't let anyone else bring you down. That doesn't mean that you don't ever listen to constructive feedback. If you've done something wrong, if you made a mistake at work and your boss needs to call you on it, you need to listen to that feedback. However, rather than focus on the wrong, on how stupid you are and how you really messed up, always approach whatever the issue is with an eye toward the solution.

If you've made a mistake, ask, "So, how can I fix it?" Approach issues from the standpoint that, "Yeah, that was messed up, but now I'm going to try and do it differently." When you're always solution oriented and focused on the future, you will have more confidence. You will see opportunity, you will see improvement, you will see growth and learning as a part of your world. Don't focus on the past; don't focus on what has been. You can focus on the lessons from the past, but don't focus on the past itself.

Avoid the Naysayers

There will always be those who tell you that you cannot do it. You are too young, too old, too experienced, too inexperienced, too this, too that, or generally not enough. They see all the obstacles to accomplishing something and can easily convince you not to try. Don't listen to them. While there is merit to identifying issues that need to be overcome, I have found that focusing on why it *can't* be done is simply not productive.

Let me tell you about a college student named Sarah. Sarah was coming to the end of her sophomore year when she came to me for help. Rather than get yet another less-than-meaningful summer job as a retail sales clerk, Sarah wanted an internship that would build her resume and skills.

There was one internship that she found that was of particular interest. Getting this would be a major coup. The internship involved working with a children's book editor at a major publishing house in New York City. She was told she did not have the experience or the background to do the job. She was told this was an internship reserved for upperclassmen only. She was told not to apply.

But she felt compelled to apply. With that goal in mind, we started discussing what qualities she had to bring to this internship and how she might best highlight those qualities. As with most job seekers, her resume and cover letter were two elements applied in conveying her branding edge. We revamped how she talked about her qualities and highlighted the skills she had used in her previous jobs. She also developed compelling signature stories for use in her interviews. She refused to give up or give in, and she got the job. Here's what she told me:

I knew exactly what I wanted to do, and for which company. I knew I wanted to be in children's book publishing and that this internship with a highly esteemed publishing company would be the perfect start. The only problem with my plan is that getting this internship—and starting my dream career—seemed impossible. I had worked a few jobs; I'd been a sales associate at a home décor store, spent a few summers as a camp counselor, and worked during the school year as an office assistant, but nothing that really seemed to translate into experience. Also, I was a year younger than everyone else applying. It felt like there were so many factors working against me, and as much as I tried to convince myself that I had a chance at this job, I had no idea how to prove it.

When I met with a career counselor at my school, she seemed to see this goal as the pipe dream of a delusional college kid. She suggested I apply for my summer camp job again, as well as applying to several other, more local, smaller establishments. Maybe she was right, maybe I was delusional, but I knew exactly what I wanted to do and only ended up applying to one job.

I honestly believe my cover letter got me that first interview. Several long discussions with Rahna finally made me realize that these seemingly useless previous jobs actually were experience, when I looked at them the right way. For example, I was a camp counselor for 4- to 7-year-olds. Whereas I knew that showed my love for kids, I hadn't thought to look from another angle: I understand what kids like, have literally been trained to think like a child and act like an adult, and know what stimulates kids' minds and makes them laugh. In the children's publishing industry, that's pretty important. My jobs as a retail clerk and office worker, on the other hand, gave me experience understanding consumers and working in an office environment. Rahna convinced me that I was the perfect person for this job and that made writing an engaging cover letter, and eventually my two interviews, a whole lot easier.

And telling my college counselor that I'd gotten this dream internship? That wasn't bad either.

Confidence Breeds Determination

Determination is a part of turbocharging your career. When I played point guard in high school basketball, my coach always admonished me to be "scrappy" and to have a sense of "stick-to-it-iveness." When you have a strong sense of what you have to offer to someone, you are much more likely to be convincing. And you are much more likely to stick with a goal until you reach it, because you have confidence in your ability to reach that goal.

Sarah could never have gotten that job if she hadn't had a core belief that she had something unique to bring to that position. She was clear about her goal and her potential contributions, and she followed a specific plan to share her vision for those contributions with the publishing house staff. Her confidence in her abilities got her that job, and that has built her resume forever. She understands her branding edge and that has effectively turbocharged her career.

Interrelated Strategies

All of these strategies are interrelated. For example, it's a lot easier to be confident if you are clear about your personal brand, you know your goal, and are taking concrete steps to achieve that goal. Each of these strategies is important. But confidence is the keystone to the arch of your career. If you don't have confidence, you will find it very difficult to sustain the energy needed to build the type of personal brand that can turbocharge your career.

Actively express your personal brand with confidence!

Chapter 6

BE PROFESSIONAL

In business, "professionalism" is not a tactic but a moral value.
—Amit Kalantri, author

Be professional. Depending on your job, being "professional" is going to mean something different to you than it will to your neighbor across the street, because he is a retail store manager and you are a teacher. If you are an accountant, then you want to be good at whatever it is that accountants need to be good at—understanding tax codes, reading balance sheets, and being data-oriented. If you're a stay-at-home mom, you need to be good at juggling crazy schedules, planning meals, and being a good cheerleader for your children.

In this chapter, we're going to talk about what is inside of you (your skills and abilities) and what is outside of you (your "packaging" and actions). It may seem as if I'm talking out of both sides of my mouth. On the one hand, your skills, abilities, and qualities are what are most important, but on the other hand, if no one is willing to discover those skills and abilities, your career engine will not be firing on all cylinders. Bear with me. Both are important, and it is the combination of the two that will truly turbocharge your career.

Be Promotable

"Be professional" essentially means that, in whatever your professional arena is, you should do a great job. Whatever you choose to spend your time doing, don't do it halfway. Don't settle for being mediocre. Be excellent. Be outstanding. Choose to be top in your field, in your office, in your company.

If you want to be an author, study the skills needed to become an *excellent* author. If you want to be in marketing, study what it is that marketers study.

My teenage son has gone to a camp in Maine ever since he was 7 years old. The camp features every fun activity you can possibly think of—rock climbing, canoeing, hiking, waterskiing, soccer, tennis, sailing, "rocks & ropes," lacrosse, basketball, kayaking, around-the-clock games of capture the flag, woodsman adventures, roasting marshmallows for s'mores, arts and crafts, and archery.

But that's not why I send him there. The counselors structure all their activities and programs around four pillars, one of which is the concept of "be your best." On Friday nights around the weekly council fire, the counselors impart wisdom by discussing this principle within the context of the daily fun they are having.

My son took this concept to heart, particularly in the area of archery and waterskiing. He wanted to perfect his skills in these areas, so he got up early (before all the other campers) to practice. In archery, he got so good that he became the first camper to "pass out" of archery (meaning that he had reached the highest level of accuracy from fifty yards away).

This principle also applies to your branding efforts. "Be your best" is about trying your hardest, doing your best in everything that you do. At camp, this translates into orderly cabins ready for daily inspection and striving for excellence in all activities. For your brand, it means putting your best foot forward and constantly improving what you bring to your marketplace.

At camp, counselors are careful to encourage a spirit of friendly competition, one that builds campers up without denigrating the others. In corporate programs that I give, I talk about being professional as a key ingredient to developing a strong personal brand that furthers your business success. You can work to "be your best" in your client dealings, in your presentations, and in your management of your teams, all the while still honoring the others on your team. Respect your talents (as well as others) and honor the fact that you do things in a unique and wonderful way. Understand that it's not a race against others; it's really an ongoing, never-ending "race" against yourself, a race between who you are and who you are going to be.

When I worked for Texaco, I stood in the pits during the races and listened to the pit crew chief and driver talking back and forth. Every second they are on the track (and even when they are off the track), they are refining their strategies, tweaking the car, and doing everything they can to squeeze more performance out of that car. The same applies to you. To turbocharge your career, you need to continually refine your personal brand.

How do you do that? Evaluate what skills you need in order to be professional. Typically, information like this comes out in an annual performance review, if your company has those. But don't wait until the annual review. Take the initiative and ask your boss what skills he would like to have you work on. He'll be blown away and think, "Wow, what a go-getter!" He'll be so excited that you want to grow and do more that he'll start taking more notice of what you already do well. The idea with personal branding is to shine a spotlight on your core competencies, and this process of just trying to be as professional as you can possibly be will do just that. It can actually spark a phenomenal conversation as, in order to ask what qualities or skills you need to add, you'll both have to assess what you already express.

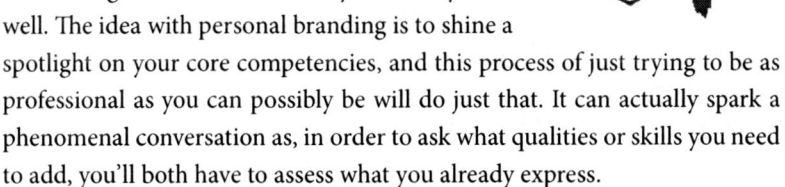

GET YOUR EDGE

20. Be what you want to be (Part I)

Make sure you understand valued skills in your industry and why they are valued. Ask yourself these questions:
- In my chosen field, what skills do I need to have in order to be professional?
- What tools do I already have in my toolbox that are valued in my company or industry?
- What skills are valued that I don't currently have? What skills would help me get to the next level of performance? What tools do I need to add to my toolkit?

Acting "As If"

If you want to get promoted, then you need to start acting like the next level up. Let's say you are a manager in the customer service center, and you want to be promoted to director. You need to start acting like a director—now. Do not wait for a promotion to be a director. I don't mean you should run around your office barking out orders to your colleagues or attending meetings to which you have not been invited. What I mean is, embody the qualities of a director. Add "director" to your personal brand. For example, if director-level people are coaching their direct reports on how to handle difficult phone calls, then be the best at answering calls. Be a resource for your colleagues; show the leadership skills that will have people naturally turning to you for guidance.

You see, one way to speed up your promotion is to be promotable. Typically, your boss has to recommend that you be promoted; make her job easy! Often, promotions are determined by committee, with everyone in the department reviewed annually. If you have a strong personal brand, everyone will simply be nodding their heads when your boss brings up your name as a candidate for promotion. It will seem only natural that you be promoted, because it's already part of your personal brand. The promotion will then simply be a formality because you are already a director in your actions, in your thoughts, in your behavior.

GET YOUR EDGE

21. Be what you want to be (Part II)

Think of someone who is currently doing what you desire to do.
- What qualities or skills do you admire about that person?
- What qualities or skills do you NOT admire?
- How can you incorporate the desirable qualities and skills into your daily life right now?

Practice, Practice, Practice

Practice makes perfect. That axiom is true in every walk of life, and it definitely holds true when it comes to the expression of your personal brand. If you want to be the best, practice. If you are giving a speech to your department or your leadership team, practice. Whatever activities need to become core to your brand, practice them!

When people think about developing and evolving their personal brand (or about more dramatic reinvention!), there is always an element of fear. They are afraid to look foolish or fake. One question I hear a lot is, "How can I express this new quality without seeming fake?" My answer: Practice. When you practice something, you naturally get better at it, and then it does not seem so foreign. When you practice something over and over and over again, you will become a "pro" at it, and that's what being professional is all about!

> *Fear is the result of a lack of confidence; and a lack of confidence is the result of not knowing what you can do; and that is caused by a lack of experience. So get a record of successful experience behind you, and your fears will vanish.*
> —Dale Carnegie, author, motivational speaker, trainer

Be Prepared

Do your job. Be ready when you are supposed to be ready. If you have a weekly meeting with your boss, be prepared for that meeting. Take the initiative to think through what you would like to accomplish from the meeting and what you believe he or she would like to accomplish from the meeting. You will be seen as a leader if you take charge of your work and your job.

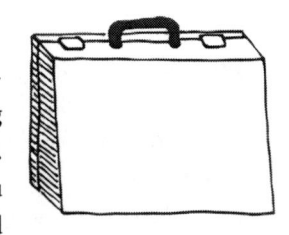

Earlier in this book, I said that you shouldn't let life happen to you. You need to make it happen. You must actively manage your job as a part of actively managing your brand.

Look the Part

A brand manager strives to maximize content—to make the best product possible, giving as much value as possible. However, he or she also needs to make sure that a consumer is willing to look in the box to see all that great content. That's why packaging is such a crucial part of any marketing efforts. The same applies to you.

So let's talk about your "packaging." When we talk about being professional, we mean conveying a certain image to your clients, to your colleagues, to your boss, to the executives in your company. You need to make sure your visual image matches the personal brand you are aiming for.

> *Dress shabbily and they remember the dress; dress impeccably and they remember the woman.*
> —Coco Chanel, fashion icon, entrepreneur, founder of the Chanel brand

Maximize Your Physical Image

You will also want to do what you can to maximize your appearance physically. This is a tricky subject, because people come in all sizes, shapes, and colors. They also come with curly, straight, balding, grey, or frizzy hairstyles and even more varied senses of style. Your mother always told you not to judge a book by its cover, and that is wise counsel, but the hard truth is that everyone does it. Like it or not, your physical appearance gives an impression of you, so you need to consider it part of the overall expression of your personal brand. Taking several factors into account—body type, hair, facial features, clothing, and general carriage—ask yourself: "How can I maximize what I have?"

The good news is that you don't necessarily have to have a flawless-skinned, tiny-waisted, six-pack ab super-body in order to be successful (unless, of course, being a fitness guru is a critical part of your personal brand, in which case, you probably already have a super-body!).

One thing that helps, especially in the area of carriage and executive presence, is to be comfortable in your own skin. If it bothers you to have grey hair, then color it! If you are super self-conscious about your skin, use whatever miracle cream works for you. We've already discussed the importance of self-worth in the previous chapter, and certainly appearance plays a role in that positive sense of self. Change and enhance what you want to, but also accept where you are even as you are trying to evolve.

I haven't been skinny since I was fourteen. When I filled out, I filled out everywhere! But it never stopped me from being a success. I bought clothes

> ### Christine's Story—Be Professional
>
> Being in the design industry, Christine really gets the concept that her physical appearance matters. She is very aware of other people's physical presence; when someone with a physical presence walks into a room, it's like a gravitational pull. As an artist, she wants people to be drawn to her, so they can take advantage of what she's offering. She is mindful of what her body language is saying and even of what she says. Here's what Christine says about being aware of her professional image:
>
> "Most eye-opening was the information you shared about the "unconscious" factors that people use when meeting someone. These factors help us decide whether we should give people our trust, our admiration, and, most useful to me, our business. Being in the design industry, I have always given great credence to "looking the part" everywhere, even the grocery store. However, knowing that other judgments are being made about my intelligence, honesty, and professional ability has made me stronger as a businesswoman."
>
> Christine needed to show her elegant creativity in every way possible. Entrepreneurs understand that you can meet your next potential client anywhere—even, as she says, while standing in line at the grocery store.
>
> But maybe you work in a corporation so you think it doesn't matter how you come across in the grocery store, until you see the president of your company there. That actually happened to me when I worked with the LEGO brand, as we lived in the same very small town. It doesn't matter if you are an entrepreneur or a corporate manager, if you want to turbocharge your career, you need to make sure you are conveying your personal brand in your physical appearance as well as in the skills you express.

that were appropriate to my size and my profession, and I continue to monitor what I eat in an effort to battle the evil and magnetic forces of gravity, age, and chocolate chip cookies. If I wanted to add "supermodel" to my personal brand, I would have to make some major modifications to get in model shape, and that would need to be a specific and significant part of my action plan. For actresses and actors, dress size is an important factor in their profession, but it probably isn't in your profession. As you check how you project your professionalism, it should be a consideration, but it should not be an excuse for why you cannot be what you want to be.

Match Your Professional Image to Your Desired Profession

Does the way you dress match your profession?

Financial planners or stockbrokers will likely wear a coat and tie or a tailored suit. They need to have their shoes shined, as that is expected of the Wall Street crowd. They need to appear buttoned-up so that when they're talking to someone about managing their money, that person feels he or she can trust that the financial specialist has the ability and the wherewithal to wisely manage money.

On the other hand, if you're in a creative field and you appeared at a meeting in a three-piece business suit, people might not think your dress and your job were a match. You would need to wear something much more stylish, much more hip or cool—great shoes or some funky earrings. Even your "business" accessories can help convey this. Is your briefcase a high schooler's backpack or a stylish tote? Think about whether it will help your personal brand to be on the cutting edge of cool so that you can convey that you are creative, that you are individualistic, that you think outside the box, that you're innovative. If that's part of your brand, you want to make sure you're visually conveying that sense of innovation and creativity. I know of one entrepreneur who was awarded a contract because of the shoes she was wearing (and no, she was not in the fashion business!).

That doesn't mean someone in the corporate environment can't have creativity as a part of his or her personal brand. On the contrary, that would probably be very valued in terms of problem solving or new product development and process innovation. That creativity would simply be expressed in a more subtle way, perhaps with a stunning scarf or a knockout

They expect a professional presentation, so they expect to see a "professional." Dress appropriately for the occasion, but don't be one of the crowd.
—Wess Roberts, author

suit. However you dress, make sure it matches the professional image you are trying to convey. Show your branding edge through your personal appearance.

You do not need to be on the cutting edge of cool (unless that is a part of your personal brand, and then you probably don't need to focus on this area anyway), but you do need to be current and relevant. In order to stay up-to-date on all the latest styles and trends, you may want to enlist others in this effort. Ask a hair stylist for his or her opinion, or ask a retail clerk for fashion suggestions. Ladies, go to a department store make-up counter and ask for a makeover (you don't have to buy everything they use on you—just buy a lipstick and consider it well worth the cost of the advice). When it comes to your physical appearance, I would not rely solely on the advice of your spouse or your mother. If they are sadly out of touch with fashion, they may see nothing wrong with your Sansabelt® slacks. While they may be honest and loving, they might not be experts in this area or the best advocates for the proper development of your personal brand.

Please don't misunderstand me. I am not advocating that you be something you are not. In Chapter 7, we'll talk about the importance of authenticity. Even as I am encouraging you to "look the part" and match your outward expression with your true brand, please know that it's what's inside your package that is most important.

GET YOUR EDGE

22. Is your appearance professional? (Part I)

Be very honest with yourself on the following:
- Does your physical appearance match what you are trying to convey?
- Are there any changes you would like to make to your physical appearance to enhance your personal brand?
- How can you develop a plan for that change?

Be Polite

Make sure that you are professional in your dealings with people and that you have a basic understanding of the protocols of your industry and polite society. Be polite. Be respectful. Always treat your colleagues, your bosses, and your co-workers with respect.

Be mindful of making a good first impression. Look someone in the eye when shaking hands and have a good firm grip (no fishy, wimpy, finger-to-finger handshake). Repeat the person's name in order to help you remember it.

GET YOUR EDGE

23. Is your appearance professional? (Part II)

Consider the following:
- Is your handshake firm (without being a death grip)?
- Are there special protocols in your industry you need to be aware of?
- Are there any social situations in which you feel unsure of yourself?
- Where might you turn for assistance in this area?

My mother grew up in the wealthy neighborhoods of Main Line Philadelphia, and she made sure that her three children knew the ins and outs of proper etiquette (so much so that my sister is now a professional etiquette coach; you can find out more about her at PoisePolishPanache.com). I was always so grateful for that knowledge of etiquette because I grew up in Greenwich, Connecticut, a bedroom community just outside New York City with just about the highest per capita income in the country (except perhaps Bel Air, California). While I did not grow up as a trust fund baby, I did often find myself at a social function at one of the seven country clubs in town. Having confidence about which fork to use first and knowing which bread plate was mine allowed me to navigate those social situations with greater ease. Early in my career, I worked in the advertising department at Texaco with predominantly male managers. While there were so many great aspects of working on such a brand, it was a bit of a culture shock for me to work with "oil men." Many of these executives had worked their way up the management ranks, starting right out of high school pumping gas and getting promoted over the years. Unfortunately, no one ever gave them lessons in etiquette, and it negatively affected how they were viewed by senior management. One regional manager was in charge of the entire Midwestern region—every Texaco gas station from the Mississippi River to the Rocky Mountains. He was very nice and very smart, but etiquette was an area of his personal brand that definitely needed some help. He did not convey the professionalism and executive presence he could have, as he simply did not have the table manners to match his executive position. I once had occasion to have dinner with him and a few other agency executives, during which he made social blunder after social blunder. Over the course of forty-five minutes, he sucked on a lemon wedge, spat some pulp (and I believe an errant seed) into his salmon, licked a cruet of salad dressing (he was catching a drip), and ate off my plate without asking. Fortunately, my mother had taught me that sometimes good manners means putting up with other people's bad manners.

    I am sad to tell you that this is all I remember of this man. Not all the good business decisions he made, not what I learned from him, only that he spat on his food.

    Do not let this be you. Be known for the good you do. Be professional.

Chapter 7

BE TRUE TO YOUR BRAND

To thine own self be true.

—William Shakespeare, playwright

What does it mean to "be true to your brand"? It means you must be consistent in expressing your brand and authentic in the delivery of your brand. These two concepts are closely related because one leads to the other. If you are authentic, you will be more consistent. Let's explore these a bit further.

Be Consistent

You must be consistent in every aspect of how you express your brand. As we discussed, a brand is the promise of a future experience. The more consistent the experience, the stronger the impression will be. We don't question whether McDonald's® will be fast, because it's always fast. It may not be your favorite restaurant, but if you want a quick meal, you may just stop there.

In the 1960s, Rosser Reeves put forth in his book *Reality in Advertising* a concept of the unique selling proposition, or USP, that is at the heart of all great marketing plan development. The critical elements of a USP:

- Unique
- Specific
- Compelling
- Simple

I would add one to that: consistent. Whatever you are, be that, over and over and over again, so that consumers don't have to think about what you stand for; they just know.

In my career, I develop marketing plans for many different products or services. In developing marketing plans, it's important to look at all the different aspects of a brand, including the media plans and the marketing messages. I look at the website and the packaging and the public relations materials and at least eighteen other consumer touch points to thoroughly evaluate a product's brand messaging. It is a rigorous process to examine all the different aspects of how someone is going to get an impression about that brand.

The visual here shows the many different ways that consumers engage with a brand. The figure in the middle represents the consumer and the arrows represent possible "touch points" of that consumer's experience with the brand. It is the brand manager's job to craft these touch points in such a way that each builds on all the other brand communications.

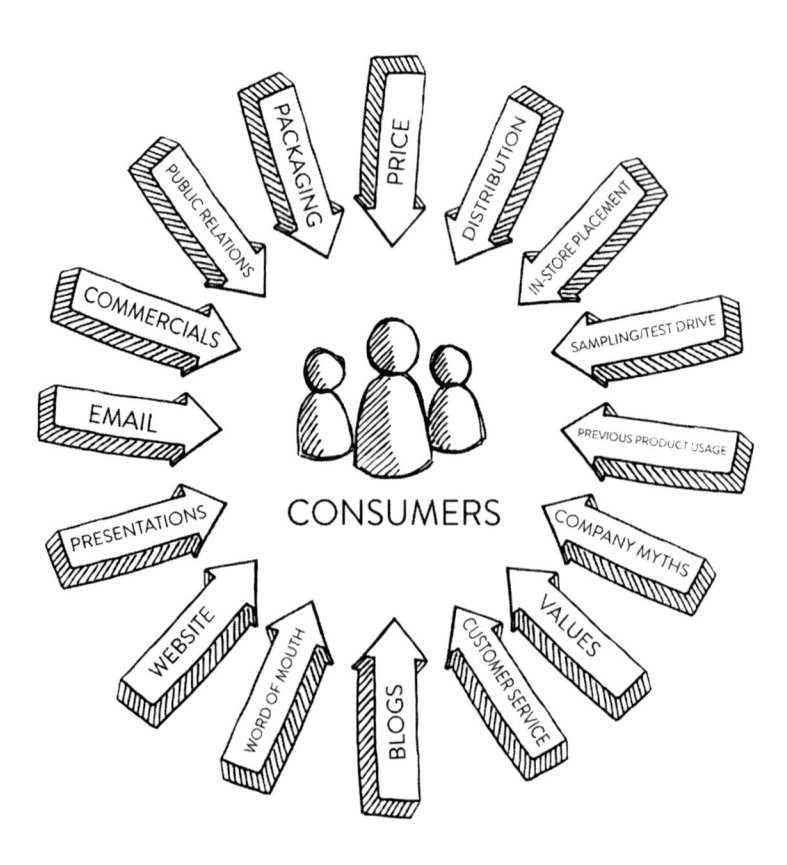

Everything that consumers hear, read, or experience about a brand influences how they think about that brand. Price communicates something about a brand automatically. What you read about in the newspaper communicates something. The type of packaging communicates something else. If you are a high-priced watchmaker and you tell someone the watch costs $5,000, that automatically brings an image to mind. That price tells something about that brand.

However, if, in your distribution, you offer that $5,000 watch at Wal-Mart, that is a departure from your brand, because you would not expect to find a premium watch in a discount store. Therefore, your brand statement is weakened because you are sending mixed messages.

Apple® is a classic example of consistent brand expression. Simplicity and innovation are at the core of this brand. These qualities were built into the DNA of the company, right from its beginning, when Steve Jobs and Steve Wozniak were driven to develop a computer that was intuitive and easy to use. When you look at how their brand gets expressed, you see simplicity and innovation *pervasive* in every aspect of their branding. Their packaging is monochromatic, and their retail stores are very clean and crisp. The billboards advertising the iPod are crisp, clean silhouettes of people with pure, white earbuds, and the iPad and iPhone rely on infinitely consumer-friendly touchscreen technology.

Identify Your Audience

A good brand manager always starts with the figure in the middle: the consumer. In branding any product or service, the brand manager would identify his target audience and seek to understand that consumer completely. He would conduct focus group research to really be sure that he understood the rational and emotional needs—as well as motivations, beliefs, and daily habits—of this audience.

Similarly, you need to identify the people you want to reach and seek to understand them. Your target audience could be your boss, your customers or clients (or potential clients), senior management in your company, your employees, an executive recruiter, your colleagues, or the industry movers and shakers. For the next two exercises, you may want to download the Target Audience Profile Worksheet available at YourBrandingEdge.com/BookExtras.

GET YOUR EDGE

24. Identify your target audiences

It's important to dive into the mindset and behaviors of the people you need to influence in order to advance your personal leadership brand. These are the key stakeholders as it relates to your personal brand. Think about the people who are somehow related to you professionally and what role they will play in the development and expression of your personal brand. Answer the following questions:

- Who are the people who have a stake in my brand—customers, co-workers, supervisors?
- Who are the influencers to those stakeholders (this could be an administrative assistant, a prominent industry leader, another business colleague, or a writer for a trade publication)?
- Who would be affected by my personal leadership brand (either positively or negatively)? These could be employees, colleagues, supervisors, mentors, industry leaders, media personnel, clients, or others who may somehow play a role in the expression of your brand.

Influences

Just as good brand managers are very consistent in their communication, you want to be consistent in the expression of your brand. In our workshops and individual coaching programs, we do a "deep dive" into personal branding influencers. Just as a product or service or company must look at all the elements affecting and shaping its brand identity, you need to spend time reviewing the factors contributing to (or detracting from) your personal brand.

When you look at this image to the right, you can see many different ways that people are getting communications about you. It's all part of actively managing your personal brand. Robin Fisher Roffer, author of *Make a Name for Yourself*, says, "If you don't make a name for yourself, someone else will!" If you don't actively manage your personal brand,

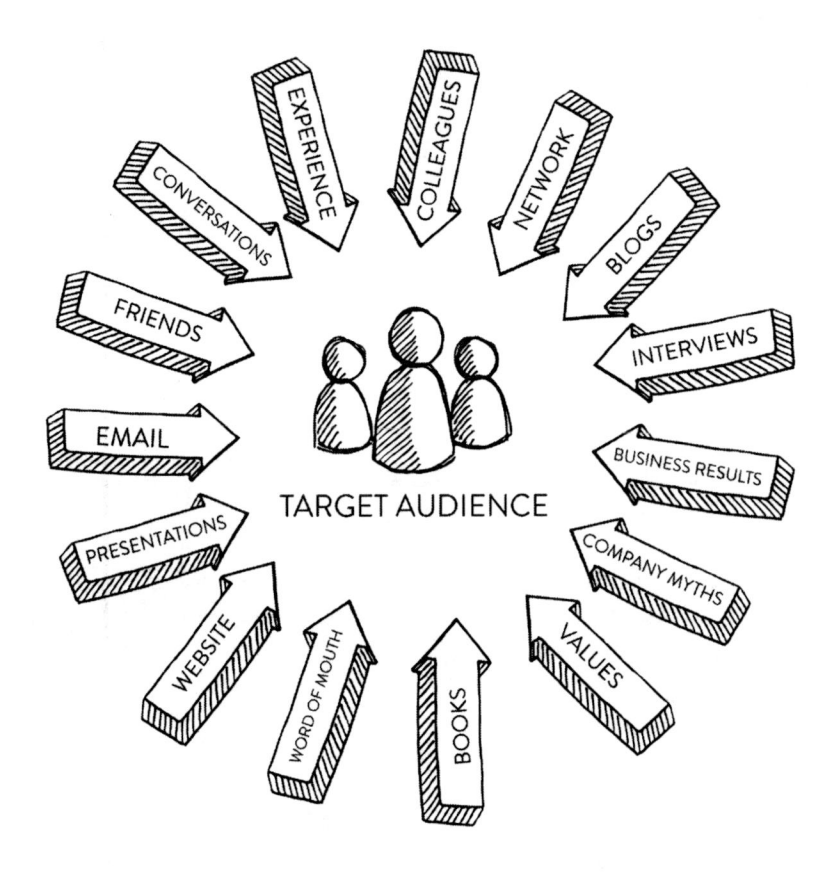

[Diagram: arrows labeled CONVERSATIONS, EXPERIENCE, COLLEAGUES, NETWORK, BLOGS, INTERVIEWS, BUSINESS RESULTS, COMPANY MYTHS, VALUES, BOOKS, WORD OF MOUTH, WEBSITE, PRESENTATIONS, EMAIL, FRIENDS pointing toward TARGET AUDIENCE at center.]

then whatever haphazardly comes across is what people will remember. Review how you are currently coming across to people and identify the activities that are working well and those that are not contributing to the personal brand you would like to express.

Be Consistent in the Delivery of Your Brand

We've talked a little bit about this in the chapter called "Be Professional." If you were going to meet with me, author of this book and chief branding strategist of Beacon Marketing, and I showed up dressed in sweats and a ratty old tee shirt, you would think there was something incongruous about me. You wouldn't believe that I was truly a competent branding consultant in the business world. I need my physical image and my position to be consistent. That's part of delivering a *consistent* message.

GET YOUR EDGE

25. Understanding your target audience

It's important to understand all the nuances of those identified target audiences. Use your imagination to put yourself in their shoes and answer the following questions:
- Who are they (describe them)?
- How do they spend their day?
- Where would you be most likely to encounter those people?
- What are they worried about?
- What are they excited about?
- What are their biggest problems?
- What are their biggest opportunities?
- What motivates them?
- Describe their rational needs* (see note below).
- Describe their emotional needs** (see note below).
- What are their current beliefs about you?
- What do they need to believe about you in order for a change to take place?

* An example of a rational need would be for someone to help analyze data in order to make recommendations for inventory changes.

** An example of an emotional need would be a feeling of greater confidence in the analysis done, a sharing of the burden of decision-making, peace of mind.

The same applies to you. You cannot be "Judy Friendly" at work and then go home and kick the dog or be super-snarky on social media sites. That's inconsistent. You need to be true to your brand, whether you're at work or at home or shopping at the mall.

And the thing is, if you are really doing those things that are core to you, you will naturally be true to your brand and you will be consistent.

Earlier, I told you that expressing your brand should be as easy as breathing. Let me give you an example of what I mean. I am a branding

GET YOUR EDGE

26. Understanding influencing factors

Think about the communication touch points shown in the arrows in the chart on page 77 and what brand statement you are making with each of those as it relates to your own personal brand. The following is a partial list of the types of influencers you need to think about and actively, purposefully manage. How have the following factors influenced what others think about you? What others can you think of? Is there any change you would like to incorporate into your desired personal brand?

- What you talk about at lunch
- The clothing you wear
- What books you read
- Your social media profiles
- Presentations you give
- The people you hang out with
- Articles you write
- Your email signature
- Your business results
- Blogs you write or comments you post
- Your voicemail message
- The projects you work on

geek. I always want to talk about, think about, and engage in branding and marketing conversations. I automatically relate everything to branding. I can be watching a Red Sox® game with my family, and I will just naturally begin to notice all that the Red Sox franchise does to promote its brand. I'll say, "Look at this *Red Sox Nation* program they have; isn't that brilliant? They gather the names of everybody who signs up to be a part of their fan club, and then they can begin a long-term conversation and relationship with those fans. Then, they can market a ton of other ancillary products and services to them. Isn't that fascinating?" At this point, my husband just rolls his eyes and asks, "Why can't you just watch the game?" The answer is that it's just part of my personal brand. I am a marketer at heart. I don't work at that; it just comes just as naturally as breathing. It drives my family crazy, but it makes me good at what I do. That's my branding edge. You want to understand what is core to *your* personal brand; that's your branding edge.

Be Authentic

In the early exercises, I asked you to find out what others think the essence of your personal brand is by asking a cross-section of people to describe you. You will probably find that some core qualities rise to the surface, because people can see your core qualities across multiple aspects of your life. It may get expressed in slightly different ways, but if you look at the responses you got, you will begin to see your authentic personal brand coming through. If you are ultra-organized at work and your desk looks "pin-perfect" as my mother would say, then I would bet money that your closet at home is organized, too. Organization would be one of the key qualities of your personal brand.

GET YOUR EDGE

27. Understanding yourself

Can you think of any topics that you are particularly passionate about? What do you never get tired of learning about?

Because of the Internet and the immediacy of social media, our age has been dubbed by many as the "'age of transparency." Our lives are so much more public now. You cannot fool people for too long. If you are being fake, eventually it's going to be discovered.

This is why some social media experts are disdainful of personal branding. It puzzles me why that is the case. It seems as though they see personal branding as a persona that you can adopt and discard, a cloak you can put on and take off at will. But that's not what true personal branding is.

Christine's Story—Be True to Your Brand

Consistency was critical to Christine, and she held everything she did to her high standards of excellence. If you visited her store, you would find it had a feel of elegance. If you visited her website, you would find rich colors and inspiring visuals that convey her couture brand. The rich feel and elegant branding was repeated in her newsletter; it conveyed a sense of her expertise and approachability all at the same time.

Christine says, "I tried to be totally consistent in my branding efforts. I was mindful of what my advertising looked like and the impression that it gave. When placing a print ad, I made sure that it did not run next to an ad for the tattoo parlor or something like that. I was very happy because it ended up running next to a call-out for a charity tea for little girls that the local hospital was sponsoring."

Whether she is teaching a sewing class or designing window treatments for a mansion, she insisted on consistency for her brand. "I don't cut corners, I don't discount my work. I'm very fast, so I try to work within my client's budgets, but I *never* have a sale!"

Her branding was consistent across channels. Her logo was printed on her business card with thermographic printing on a rich 100-pound heavy weight paper. Her name was on the card in red (the same red as on two of the walls of her studio). The logo on that card looked just like the sign outside of her studio. "When I handed them to people, they couldn't help but run their hands all over them. They kept rubbing their fingers on them, and that conveyed something about my brand. Being in a tactile industry, my clients are very 'touchy' people. When I design drapes for them, we get into the nitty-gritty; I will talk with them about how the drapes will feel in their hands when they pull them closed. The consistency of those details really does matter."

If you are in the corporate world, you may not have as much control over what your business cards look like, but there are plenty of other "touch points" that you do have control over. Be consistent in the delivery of your personal brand.

Your Personal Brand Emanates from Within

Authentic personal branding is being true to who you are and then setting a plan in place to shine a spotlight on what you are all about so that others can more clearly recognize your personal brand. Blogging, Facebook®, LinkedIn,® and other web 2.0 tools are simply modern-day vehicles to convey that brand. We'll talk more about how you can authentically convey your personal brand online in Chapter 9, "Be Connected."

The disdain that some have for personal branding stems from the unscrupulous practice of manipulating one's image (either online or off) in an inauthentic manner. Being true to your brand is not a new concept. A mentor once told me that the quickest way to kill a bad product is to advertise it. The same holds true with people. If you are one way online and another way in person, you will be found out—at the speed of the Internet.

> *Be yourself;*
> *everybody else is*
> *already taken.*
> —Oscar Wilde, writer, journalist, poet

Lack of Consistency and Authenticity Can Kill Your Brand

Just ask Tiger Woods.

Because Woods was such a dominant media figure, sweeping onto the golfing world at a young age and then having the staying power to win over and over again, he built up a very well-known and seemingly consistent personal brand. He portrayed massive competitiveness, drive, determination, single-mindedness, and focus. That's what we saw on the golf course, and that's what was promoted in commercials, print ads, and airport billboards by his many corporate sponsors.

In addition, the game of golf has its own brand. In golf, you have to be honest and "tell on yourself" when you are keeping score. When you are on the green, you don't walk in someone else's line before they putt, and there is a definite etiquette about who hits first off every tee and who putts first on every green. Golfing fans believe this is a gentleman's game, one of integrity and respect for others. These overarching brand qualities "rubbed off" on Woods' personal brand to form a very powerful, very public image.

So when the truth of his infidelities came out, the golfing world (and beyond) was stunned by the inconsistency. It did not fit their perception of Woods, and it has dramatically affected his career. Even as he has returned to the PGA Tour, he's not the same and he is not viewed the same.

Your Environment and Your Personal Brand

Although I highly encourage you to add skills and qualities to your brand, you cannot be something you are not. Make sure you express your brand and grow your brand in ways that are true to who you are. For example, if you don't really care about the environment, then trying to get a job at a green company out of desperation is not going to be conducive to your thriving. If you are shy and quiet and you find yourself in an atmosphere where everyone parties a lot, you may not find it easy to turbocharge your career in such an environment.

In order to keep their jobs, people will often do things that are not part of their personal brand in order to please other people. While this may work in the short term, eventually it will not allow you to reach your full potential. In order to turbocharge your career, you have to be true to your brand. Make sure the actions you take are in keeping with your personal brand, your personal ethics, and your personal values.

Your Personal Brand and Your Company's Brand

No matter where you work, there is a direct connection between your personal brand and your company brand, and this is an important factor for you to consider in the development of your personal brand. The interplay between the two is real and tangible, and the impact is reciprocal. By that I mean that the company brand affects you, and your personal brand affects the company.

This has definitely been true in my own career. When I would mention that I worked for The LEGO Group, people's eyes would light up, and they would tell me about the latest creation their children had made or share a fond memory from their own childhood experiences. People have an expectation about the LEGO brand that carries over to the people who work there. People felt that if I worked for this iconic brand, I must be creative and fun, as these are qualities embodied in the company brand. In this way, the company brand "rubbed off" on me.

GET YOUR EDGE

28. Understand your values

Think about these questions:
- What is important to you?
- What values do you hold dear in your work? In your personal life?

The same is true going the other way; your personal brand will "rub off" onto the company brand. Think about it for a minute. When the FedEx® guy shows up at the office to pick up and drop off packages, he is communicating something about the company's image. At that time, *he is* FedEx. If he is cheerful and efficient, then you will think that FedEx is a great company—efficient in its service and pleasant to work with. If he is grumpy, complaining, and unorganized, this will negatively affect your perception of the company.

As you explore and expand your own brand, you will need to understand the impact of the other brands that surround you, most notably the company brand. A good brand manager will look to associate his or her brand with other strong brands that share the same values, the same target audience, and compatible brand images. You will want to do the same.

If you are a leader in a company, you will want to consider this concept from another perspective. What do your employees convey about you? How can you leverage this in a positive way? I conduct training seminars to help companies work through this very issue. I start by bringing the concept of personal branding to everyone's attention. I then help people map out ways to have a greater positive impact on the company's business. This process has multiple effects. First, it heightens the employees' awareness of their impact so they are more mindful of how they behave with others. Second, it acts as a catalyst for change, if needed. Some employees may be unaware of how they have been potentially negatively affecting the business with their behaviors. Third, it empowers employees, who begin to see that they and their actions can make a difference and contribute to a greater whole.

GET YOUR EDGE

29. Understanding your organization

When thinking about the best work for you and where you would like to share your talents, it's important to think about where you are right now. Here are some questions to ask yourself:
- How would you describe your company's brand?
- How do they present themselves to the marketplace?
- If the company were a person, what type of person would it be?
- Is that a person you would want to hang out with?
- Are you proud to work there?
- Do other people respect this company?
- What is the culture like?
    - How does it mesh with your personal style?
    - Are there any disconnects with your style?
- What are the biggest issues affecting the company right now?
- What are the biggest opportunities for the company right now?
- Do you like this company?
    - Why or why not?
- What is the company passionate about?
- What does your association with this company say about you?
- Does it fit your personal brand? Why or why not (be as specific as possible)?

This same branding principle holds true for your industry, as well. If someone tells you he is a lawyer, a whole host of qualities and emotions spring to mind, just as it does if someone told you she works for a nonprofit government agency.

If Your Brand Conflicts with Your Company's Brand

If you are in conflict about your work environment, you need to determine whether you can change the environment or not. Then you

GET YOUR EDGE

30. Company and personal brand match

Reflect upon your current company environment as you answer the following questions.
- What do your employees convey about you?
- How can you leverage this in a positive way?
- What is the company passionate about?

may need to make the hard decision to find another job. While this may seem drastic, I promise you that when you are true to who you are, your career will thrive. I speak from personal experience here. At one point, I worked in a very demanding corporate environment with a leadership team driven by a philosophy of fear and intimidation. The job had a great deal of cachet, and I was working on a high-profile brand…But I was miserable. I didn't agree with the way the top executives treated others, and I certainly didn't appreciate how they treated me. It didn't fit with my philosophy of partnership and collaboration and, eventually, I had to leave. It took a great deal of courage to leave, and I worried that I had made a major career misstep. But I can tell you that once I left that situation, I was much happier. I started to do work that was incredibly rewarding—for my heart and my bank account. Later, I found out that many others got the courage to leave, too.

In this age of transparency, authenticity matters a lot, and, in order to turbocharge your career, you must be true to your brand, whatever your brand is.

GET YOUR EDGE

31. Understanding influencing factors

Think through your company's or industry's brand and what implications that has for your personal brand. When thinking about the best work for you and where you would like to share your talents, it's important to think about where you are right now. Think about your immediate industry, as well as the broader industry that you operate in. For example, "commercial real estate" might be the immediate industry, while "real estate" would be the broader industry in which you operate.

- How would you describe your industry's brand?
- How does it present itself to the marketplace?
- If the industry were a person, what type of person would it be?
- Is that a person you would want to hang out with?
- Are you proud to work in that industry?
- Do other people respect this industry?
- What is the culture like?
    - o How does it mesh with your personal style?
    - o Are there any disconnects with your style?
- What are the biggest issues affecting the industry right now?
- What are the biggest opportunities for the industry right now?
- Do you like this industry?
    - o Why or why not?
- What is the industry passionate about?
- What does your association with this industry say about you?
- Does it fit your personal brand? Why or why not (be as specific as possible)?

Chapter 8

BE CONNECTED

Networking is not an event or an activity; it's a strategy for life.
—Kathy McAfee, author, speaker, presentation coach

Business networking has become more and more of a buzzword and for good reason. Today's ultra-networked world makes this principle easier to apply than ever before. Networking is a critical part of any personal brand and certainly a key aspect of turbocharging your career. You want people to know who you are and what you're all about, and you can do that in person, on the phone, at a networking event, or even digitally.

How does your career advance? It is *always* through people—bosses who promote you, clients that hire you, consumers who buy from you, customers who rave about you, people who see and acknowledge your value. So it stands to reason that it's crucial to be connected with other people and to communicate with them in order to benefit from having a really strong personal brand.

When I went away from home for my freshman year in college, my mother wrote me a letter, admonishing me not to be shy, to reach out and discover all the wonderful qualities that other people express. She wrote, "Find the gold in others—and then start banking with it!" That is really what networking is all about—discovering that wonderful things happen when you genuinely like other people and express kindness to them.

The first part of my mother's admonition is about seeing the good in others. One of the wonderful benefits of public speaking is that

I get to meet a lot of people, and they all have amazing gifts to give to this world. People truly are wonderful, and there is an emotional and spiritual richness that comes from having a strong network.

But there can also be a monetary benefit that comes from being connected. That's the second part of my mom's wisdom. There are tangible benefits to your career when you have a strong network. If you want to turbocharge your career, then turbocharge your relationships.

Be Authentic

You can't do this in a phony way. The principles of networking are grounded in the same principles of authenticity we talked about in the last chapter. You must approach networking with authenticity and sincerity. When you engage with others, do not approach it from the standpoint of "getting" only. If you do, you may meet a lot of people, but you will not create advocates or fans. Eventually, your self-centeredness will be discovered.

Nadira's Branding Edge

As a world-record-holding runner, Nadira Fuller was a heavily recruited athlete in high school and got a full scholarship to the University of Florida. Her whole life consisted of eating, running, sleeping, running, studying, running, and then a whole lot more running. Running was her life, and she spent all her time at the track—working out, running, stretching, training, and then hanging out with the team between athletic events. At highly competitive schools such as the University of Florida, athletic advisors are assigned to high-talent athletes to help them integrate and deal with the rigors of college life and the physically demanding schedule of a Division I NCAA athlete.

But deep inside of her was an artist yearning to come out, and Nadira was determined to pursue that passion. Those athletic advisors discouraged Nadira from choosing a design major because of the many hours required in the studio to draw, paint, and create. But she was determined to follow her heart and, while she continued to love running, she found the time spent in the studio fed her soul.

Nadira followed her passion and was true to her brand, and this led to some career-altering connections for her. One day, she had been working out by running up and down the stairs at the football stadium. She saw a photographer taking pictures and engaged him in conversation about design and style and having an artistic eye. The photographer turned out to be Geoffrey White, a top photographer for *Sports Illustrated*. He was there doing a story on the football team. Because he enjoyed the conversation with Nadira, he asked if she would like to work as his assistant for the weekend. She agreed, and that was the start of a very long-standing professional relationship with him. She ended up acting as his assistant several times throughout the course of her college career. Because she was bold enough to start an authentic conversation about something she loved and was willing to get connected, she turbocharged her career.

When it came time to graduate, that photographer was instrumental in helping her land an internship with Sports Illustrated in New York. From that internship, she was able to secure a position at a graphic design firm, where she worked for many years. Nadira continues to connect with others through the world of art. As a matter of fact, she gave input on the design of the cover of this book! These days, she is expressing her talents in the digital world at A Drawing Project (adrawingproject.com). Go there to check out her artistic explorations.

So how can you benefit from being connected? Let's talk about some specific ways that you can strengthen your personal brand and your career by being connected.

Start with People You Know

Think about your various networks. You have a network of friends, family, and business colleagues, as well as your community network. These people experience your personal brand on a regular basis. All of these networks can be interconnected and can help you strengthen and deliver your personal brand to a wide audience.

My good friend, Kathy McAfee, author of *Networking Ahead for Business* says, "Networking allows you to grow your sphere of influence in order to manage your career, create new business opportunities, and increase your personal influence in the world. This can be done by accessing three major spheres of your network: your active network, your lost network, and your future network." She is a master networker and helps others break down their networking efforts into manageable chunks. Think about each of these networks and identify those whom you value and those whom you can help. Kathy recommends that you identify a "Top 50" list of your inner circle of people with whom you network, and then suggests you contact them at least once every five weeks or so. If you want more networking tips, visit her website, AmericasMarketingMotivator.com.

GET YOUR EDGE

32. Identify your network (Part I)

Write down at least ten people in each of the following areas of your life who are important to you. These people represent the key networks that make up the fabric of your life. At this point, you are brainstorming, so you want to generate as many names as you can.
- Family
- Business/professional people (people you work with, people in your industry, your clients, mentors, mentees, employees)
- Friends
- Community (church members, baseball coach, your daughter's piano teacher)

Your Past and Future Networks

You should also think about two particular "sub-sets" of your network that Kathy McAfee advocates: your "lost" network and your "future" network. Your lost network consists of those people who *used* to be in your inner circle (colleagues from your previous job, people from the neighborhood where you used to live, your college buddies). There may be some in that lost network with whom you'd like to reconnect.

Your future network is composed of those with whom you'd like to have a relationship. Part of your action plan should be to figure out whom you would like to add to your list of contacts and strategize a plan for meeting those people.

GET YOUR EDGE

33. Identify your network (Part II)

Write down at least ten people in each of the following areas of your life:
- Your past network (those you would like to re-connect with)
- Your future network (those you would like to connect with)

Who Knows You?

Some people say that it's not who you know, but who knows you that is important. Personally, I think they are both important. If you are going to contribute, you will need to refer your friends and family to people who can help them, which means you need to know other people.

Personal branding is a form of marketing yourself, becoming known by others for your strengths and value. Strong personal branding helps your career because it paves the way for opportunities to come to you. So expand the list of people who know you and the value you can bring.

When I worked at Texaco, I spent a fair amount of time on the racetracks across America. In NASCAR and other racing venues, there is a concept known as "drafting." One car will pull in tight behind another car to take advantage of the aerodynamic draft created by the lead car. The cars behind the lead car are literally pulled long by an unseen air current, which increases fuel efficiency and speed. Everyone benefits from this practice, even the lead car. Often, you will see many cars drafting around the track this way. Drivers may "hang out" behind a lead car, waiting for the right opportunity to step out from behind the lead driver. When the second car pulls out from the lead car, the aerodynamic forces act like a slingshot, catapulting that second car ahead for just a moment. That little extra push is often used to competitive advantage for many an exciting split-second photo finish.

In your career, you may know people you would like to draft with, those who can smooth the way ahead until you are ready to catapult into greatness. And remember, in drafting (and in personal branding), you are looking for the situations in which everyone wins. The more strong personal brands there are, the more everyone benefits!

GET YOUR EDGE

34. Who can you draft with?

> Think of people you might be able to draft with, people whom you consider to be key influencers in your industry, your company, or your world. These are people who seem to know everyone, who are the "movers and shakers" in your field. Also, think about whether they know you and, if not, how they might get to know you. What do you have to offer them?

Who Are Your Close Connections?

Any discussion of crafting your personal brand must include a discussion of your connections. Your associations affect your personal brand in several ways. They create an image, certainly, but they also have an impact on what you know. By hanging out with like-minded people—those interested in what you are interested in—you will learn what they know. It will feed your mind and feed your soul, as you will totally enjoy the conversations with these people. If you want to be a singer, hang out with other singers to find out how they do what they do. If you want to be a carpenter, hang out with other carpenters to find out how to develop the skills they have. You want to learn from the people who already do what you want to do.

Let's say you want to learn to complain less, to become more positive. One strategy to help you accomplish this goal would be for you to hang out with very positive, enthusiastic people. This can be a pretty big challenge, but actively placing yourself in the kind of situations you want to be in will speed your progress toward the accomplishment of those goals.

> ### Christine's Story—Be Connected
>
> Even though Christine was not a native to the town she lived in, she learned to identify other businesses that were serving the same types of people she served and draft with them. Says Christine, "I remembered our conversations about networking, partnering with people, and the importance of prominent placement, and that definitely helped me build my brand. Aligning with the owner of the upscale, New York–style hair salon was really a big break for me. She turned out to be a key influencer, as hairdressers are like bartenders—they know everyone in town! This woman is a successful businesswoman who is very well respected in the community. That really launched me as a newcomer in town.
>
> "I learned the importance of aligning only with those whose values matched my brand values. Before I started the course at the Entrepreneurial Center, I had offered to partner with a local "off-the-rack" curtain store. It allowed her to add custom curtains to her pre-packaged offerings, but there just was not a strong synergy there. I got two clients from it, but she was really not able to sell my work. It was difficult for me, because I *wanted* to teach her how to sell this product, but it just didn't work. It was not in keeping with my brand and the couture windows I was becoming known for, so I found a gracious way to end that association."
>
> Christine had cracked the code on "finding the gold in others—and then banking with it!" Her relationships were strategic and authentic, true to what she is and what she does. That's part of her branding edge.

Your Turbocharging Connections

Each of the people you identified in assignments 32–34 has the potential to be critical in the development of your brand in many different ways. Realize there are many roles your network members can play. For example, some may help teach you a new skill, while others will be the ones you "practice" your new skills on. Someone else may introduce you to the right people you need to meet. Some will simply support you in your efforts to make a difference. My mother is not particularly influential in the traditional sense; she is not famous, nor is she a celebrity. But she is a creative, loving support to me, and my relationship with her is extremely valuable.

GET YOUR EDGE

35. Identify your turbocharging connections

Begin to prioritize your turbocharging connections. These are the people who are critically important to your success, relationships that you are *committed* to nurturing through active engagement.
- Begin to outline what role each of these people plays in your life. The question to ask yourself is, "Who are the key people in my life that already have a big impact on me and can be leveraged to help me achieve my goals?"
- If you are using the personal branding workbook available at YourBrandingEdge.com/BookExtras, you will want to put these names into the "Who" column, then identify the "Why" of your relationship with those people.
- Think about the mutual value that exists—what they provide you and what you provide them. The "why" will vary with each person—I've seen "great contacts," "common goals," "idea exchange," "inspiration," "laughter," "motivation," "mutual admiration," even "mutual survival." This should go in the "Why" column of the turbocharging connections exercise.

Digital Networking

The world of networking has undergone a revolution in recent years. Harnessing the power of the Internet is a key way for you to connect with others and turbocharge your career. Anything you ever wanted to learn about is out there and many of the people you would like to connect with are out there, too. And you should be out there as well. To make the connections and build the relationships you want to build, all you have to do is search the web. Join a chat, participate on a blog, engage in a community. You'll become known by others who will associate you with your topic; your personal brand will blossom.

The Internet has become a critical career-builder and a vital part of any personal branding plan for several reasons:
- It offers a vehicle for self-expression through blogging and social media.
- It offers a way to find others interested in what you are interested in.
- It allows others to find you.

Those who contribute to the digital world benefit from its rich rewards. The number of technological tools available to us today to help us manage and stay current with all of our various networks is staggering. Social networking sites, the blogosphere—all these tools facilitate ongoing connections that help us deliver our brand to myriad audiences.

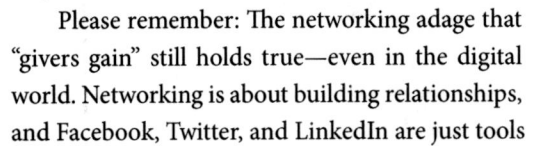

Please remember: The networking adage that "givers gain" still holds true—even in the digital world. Networking is about building relationships, and Facebook, Twitter, and LinkedIn are just tools to help make that happen faster and more broadly, while at the same time in a more targeted fashion.

You have to make yourself easy to find and easy to access, and social networking sites can provide a good way to do that. As a part of your personal branding action plan, you may want to get more engaged in the digital world—sign up for a Twitter account, post a YouTube video—do something! There may be specific industry associations or networking groups related to your particular field or area of expertise. You'll want to get connected in those areas as well.

Building Your Brand Online

If you already have an established digital presence, take a hard look at your various social media and blogging profiles. These are areas that have a dramatic impact on your personal brand. As a good brand manager, actively manage your personal brand on the worldwide web. When

Facebook first came out, it was strictly for college students and carried far too many pictures of drunken, double-fisted beer-drinking Mardi Gras party photos. Eventually, all those kids graduated from college and wanted to maintain contact with their network even after they moved into the business world, so Facebook has become much more mainstream.

Some people like to keep their profiles separate and private, and you can do that. The more private you are, the harder it will be for people to find you, and you may want that control. However, be careful of depending too much on privacy settings to keep your private image away from the public eye. Because Facebook keeps updating its privacy settings, it's harder and harder to manage your image in that way. In addition, I'm still a proponent of being who you are—everywhere. You need to be authentically you, but you want to project the best you that you possibly can in a wider arena. Understand that the first thing a prospective client or employer is going to do is type in your name on a favorite search engine. Does your online brand match with what you would like to be known for in the future? Is your profile indicative of the kind of brand that you want to project? If you want to be known as trustworthy, how would you project that on your LinkedIn account? Would you really tweet that comment if you knew it was going to be read by your boss?

If you want to be known for doing Excel spreadsheets, post something about that activity on appropriate social media sites. Write a blog or LinkedIn post to tell someone what you are doing. The beauty of social networking is the power of leverage, the power of one-to-many. You post something once, but it goes out to everybody that likes your Facebook fan page or those following you on Twitter.

Short and sweet can get you noticed. Twitter is 140 characters, so it's not a big deal. It's just a one-liner, but as soon as you send it out, people who are "following" you or "linked" with you are now aware of what you can offer. If your offering meets their needs, they may be inclined to give you a call. And if your message is forwarded on to others (or retweeted), your influence can grow exponentially.

Technology Only Facilitates Human Engagement

One common misconception about social networking is that it is all about gaining followers. Absolutely not. There are definitely people who are

GET YOUR EDGE

36. Review your social media profile and activies

- Google your name. See what comes up and what message is being communicated. Is it conveying what you'd like? Revise your website or social networking profiles as necessary.
- Set up a (free) Google Alert for your name and a few other relevant terms. This could be your client's if you are a sales person or your company if you are an entrepreneur.
- Find out if others in your field are more likely to be on Face book, Twitter, LinkedIn, or some other social network. Let your business area drive which sites you use to establish a presence.

actively trying to get as many followers as possible, but that's not what I'm talking about. I'm talking about engaging in a community digitally to share interests, learn from each other and about each other, and *connect*—just as we humans did before we had a keyboard on every desk. Please remember that it is still about connecting human to human, and while technology can aid in streamlining that, it cannot replace human interaction.

That's how it works. So if you want to build your personal brand, you can do so digitally on LinkedIn, Facebook, Pinterest, Twitter or any of the other social media arenas that continually crop up.

Other Ways to Establish Yourself Digitally

Depending on whether you are in a corporate situation or working as an entrepreneur, you may or may not need a website or a blog (or perhaps a hybrid blog website). Both of these require that you make a larger investment in your online presence. If you are going to blog, you need to do so on a regular basis (or set up a system where others have joined you in creating content on a regular basis). You may want to start by posting a comment on someone else's blog; you can still become known within a digital community without have to commit to a blog yourself.

GET YOUR EDGE

37. Identify your top digital networking strategies

Write down some key ways that you plan to communicate your brand online.
- What amount of time and energy will you put into such vehicles?
- Identify some blogs or online destinations where your industry congregates.

Please understand that building your digital presence is such a much larger topic than can be covered in this one chapter. Get started and jump in!

Using Technology to Connect in Old-fashioned Ways

Some people find it daunting to think about staying in contact with fifty people every five weeks. How can this possibly be accomplished in our busy lives? The answer lies in technology. Certainly, as we've just described, the advent of social media has made it easier to stay connected. But don't forget all the other tools you have at your disposal to be connected and actively manage your personal brand. Have you posted anything on YouTube? What does your email signature say about you? Have you listened to your outgoing voicemail message lately? What impression does it create? How do you use your cell phone? These brilliant pieces of technology allow us to call or text people while waiting at the airport or standing in line. Each interaction you have with people is adding to (or detracting from) your personal branding edge.

In addition, there are other technological tools you can use. I like to reach out in kindness to others by sending a card in the mail. My mother always admonished me to write thank you notes and send Christmas cards to important people in my life. Thank you cards can be a critical component to turbocharging you career. Joe Girard was known as the man who sold the most cars in America because he sent birthday cards to all of his customers, and Mary Kay Ash, founder of Mary Kay® Cosmetics and one of the most respected entrepreneurs of all time, sent out three thank you cards a night before she went to bed. Sending a card after meeting a client or having coffee with someone is a great way to stay in touch in a highly branded way.

But who has time to personalize all those cards? I found an online service that allows you to create cards with your own photos or logos and customize those cards with your own handwriting and signature, all at an extremely low price. I create the cards online, and the company will print it, stuff it, stamp it, and put it in the mail for me. All the benefits of personal branding combined with the technological leverage of the Internet! (If you'd like more information on this card service, check out the resources page at YourBrandingEdge.com/Resources).

Be Relevant

Being connected also means being connected to what is going on in your industry, your department, or your area of expertise. When I learn about new social media options, I am staying connected to my industry (marketing) by continuing to learn about social media. You need to stay connected to your industry to stay on top of trends. Keep learning and growing and adding to your personal brand (we'll talk more about that in the next chapter).

Expressing Yourself Across Your Networks

As we have discussed, you want to express your personal brand to as wide an audience as possible and understand that you're going to express your unique qualities, your unique gifts, to different groups of people at different times and in slightly different ways.

The problem-solving you do at work may be applied to challenges with growing businesses or averting mishaps or skillfully managing clients. When you apply your problem-solving skills at home, it may be working out a difficult schedule, taking your son to hockey practice while your daughter

> *Networking is not about just connecting people. It's about connecting people with people, people with ideas, and people with opportunities.*
> —Michele Jennae, author and entrepreneur

has a parent-teacher conference and your husband needs to be at a business meeting.

If you're a numbers person, you will find ways to express that talent in lots of different arenas. You're an accountant at work, the one who pays the bills at home, and the treasurer at your church. If you are highly creative, you're creative in lots of different ways, and if you want to become known for being creative, find as broad an audience as possible. Just understand that your core competencies, your personal brand, will get expressed in multitudinous ways in your life.

GET YOUR EDGE

38. Plan how you will reach your turbocharging connections

Go back to the assignment on identifying turbocharging connections and write down how you plan to network with these important people. Capture some thoughts about ways that you can engage on an ongoing basis with those identified (phone, face-to-face meetings). For those in your "future" network, think about how you could possibly meet that person. If you are using the Turbocharging Connections worksheet available at YourBrandingEdge.com/BookExtras, you would add this information to the "How" section of the networking sheets.

Chapter 9

BE BOLD

We are here! We are here! We are here!
—The Whos of Whoville from *Horton Hears a Who* by Dr. Seuss

In order to have a very strong personal brand, you need to be bold. You need to live out loud and let the world know you are here. In short, you need a marketing plan. The major aspects of a marketing plan include *what* you communicate, *where* you communicate it and *how* you communicate it. *What* you communicate is the main "marketing message," *how* you communicate is the strategy and the *where* is the "media plan" or the channels you'll use to convey your marketing message.

Be Your Own Best Advocate

Truly, you must be *strategically* visible. If you take the time to understand your brand, discover who you are, and really identify what is unique about you, terrific. It is important work, and it must be done. But that's only the first step. If you don't tell anyone what you do, what you want to do, and what you are passionate about, it will not help your career. Millions impacted by the widespread downsizing of America learned that you cannot rely on someone else to manage your career for you. It's up to *you*. If you think managing your career means you can sit in your cubicle, do a good job, go home at the end of the day, and take comfort in the fact that your boss says "thank you," you are sadly mistaken. You need to be your own best advocate. You are worth more focus and effort than what others will give you, and you deserve the chance to make the biggest contributions possible to your world.

There are lots of programs that help you find your purpose or discover your strengths. They may help you understand the career paths you should be pursuing. But the concepts presented here are different because I believe that you have to *do something* with that knowledge. This chapter will guide you through the basic steps for developing a marketing plan for yourself. As brand manager of your personal brand, it's up to you to increase awareness about what contributions you are making and create greater visibility for yourself. You need to create your branding edge by having a specific plan in place for how you can communicate, how you can get your personal branding message out there. The growth, development, raises, promotions, bonuses, exposure, and other recognition you seek do not come from *understanding* your brand; those benefits come from *communicating* your brand to others. If you want to turbocharge your career, you must be bold.

> *When you can do a common thing in an uncommon way, you will command the attention of the world.*
> —George Washington Carver, scientist, educator, inventor

Build a Lighthouse

I believe that your brand acts as a lighthouse, shining out to everyone who needs what you have to offer. It should serve as the foundation and guiding force for your career. You've got to stand out in order to get ahead. A strong personal brand can serve as your ultimate navigational aid, guiding your career growth. It shines out to others who can then see what you are all about, and it attracts employers, promotions, and opportunities.

How bright is your light? How strong is your tower? That's what this book is all about, building your lighthouse as big as possible. Having a strong personal brand brings opportunities and shields you from career setbacks. If your brand is built on solid rock, you'll be able to weather any storm, no matter what the economic situation. People with strong personal brands are impervious to the crashing waves of layoffs, restructuring, and economic fluctuations. That is not to say that someone with a strong personal brand may never get laid off. It still could happen. However, if you have a really bright light, it will shine beyond your own company and out to your industry. Other companies may need just what you have to offer and be delighted that you are now available.

In order to build such a lighthouse, you must be bold. You need to express your brand to as wide an audience as possible. There are myriad ways to increase your visibility, and this is the critical work that will turbocharge your career beyond what you can imagine. There are "old-school" methods to increasing your visibility, as well as new technologies that can be leveraged to get you out there in bigger and better ways. Thanks to the Internet, it is easier to see and be seen than ever before.

Start with Your Target Audience

A good brand manager starts with a focus on the target audience. Everything emanates from that, so make sure you have done the exercise of identifying your target audience

GET YOUR EDGE

> Make sure you have identified your primary and secondary audiences from the exercises in the previous chapter. The primary target audience will be individuals who have the largest influence on achieving your objectives. Behind that, the secondary audience should also be identified and incorporated into your action planning process.
>
> If you'd like help exploring your target audience and what motivates them, check out the target audience worksheet at YourBrandingEdge.com/BookExtras.

Think about Your Professional Arena

Your professional arena provides boundaries for the development of your personal brand. Although it can be expressed as the category in which you operate, it could also be something broader than that. Examples of your professional arena could be:

- Real estate agent
- Vice president of sales
- Marketing consultant
- Social media guru
- Accountant
- Executive coach
- Seamstress
- Packaging engineer

If you want to refine the professional arena, you could get more specific and more descriptive:

Real estate agent	becomes	first-time homebuyer specialist
Vice president of sales	becomes	results-driven leader
Marketing consultant	becomes	consumer engagement advocate
Social media guru	becomes	chief digital marketer
Accountant	becomes	QuickBooks expert
Executive coach	becomes	senior management motivator
Seamstress	becomes	fabric genius
Packaging engineer	becomes	master of boxes

GET YOUR EDGE

39. Identify your professional arena

Start by writing down your title or general job description. Then brainstorm more creative, more specific ways to describe what you do.

Understanding Higher-Order Benefits

The next step is to determine the unique benefits you bring to your professional arena. Why you? What values will others get from having you do what you do?

One of the mistakes people often make is to focus on features, not benefits. In personal branding, it is important not just to talk about the functional activities you engage in but also to really get to the emotional "higher-order" benefits of engaging you versus someone else.

In traditional product or service branding, brand managers discover and highlight the "higher-order benefits" their brand provides. Early on in my career, I learned a laddering technique to get to those higher-order benefits.

For more than nineteen years, Michelin ran a campaign picturing a baby in a tire that carried the tagline, "Because so much is riding on your tires." I can imagine the conversation in the conference room with the engineers at the Michelin Tire Company. They were probably all excited about steel-belted cable technology, eagerly explaining how cool this technology was, with a series of seven cables wrapped around two cables that was wrapped around one center cable. When the marketing team looked blankly at the engineers, they would have explained that this technology gave the tire its strength. Now this "seven wrapped around two wrapped around one" explanation isn't very exciting to most consumers. Consumers just want to know that their tires work. So the marketing team had to turn this dry technical feature into a benefit that consumers can get excited about.

Here's how it is done. Starting with the feature of steel-belted cable technology, they could ask themselves the question, "What's so good about that?" or "So what?" This is called a **laddering exercise** and it is a traditional form of developing the higher-order benefits for use in advertising.

"What's so good about this technology?"
It's high-tech.
"What's so good about that?"
That gives me better control and better handling of the car.
"What's so good about that?"
That gives me better performance in my car.
"What's so good about that?"
My car performs like a racecar.

Owning a car that performs like a racecar gets to the emotional needs of consumers.

Another angle of this laddering exercise shows that the same steel-belted cable technology also means the tires are stronger.

"What's so good about that?"
It means there's less wear and tear, so my tires last longer.
"What's so good about that?"
It lets me save the money.
"What's so good about that?"
That means that I'm going to spend my money wisely.
"What's so good about that?"
It makes me feel smart.

Result: that same "less wear and tear" feature and the fact that these tires last longer also means that the tires are more reliable.
"What's so good about that?"
It means that the tires are safe.
"What's so good about that?"
Well, that gives me peace of mind.

By the time the Michelin marketing team had done this laddering exercise, they could see that there were several different ways they could go. They could have a campaign that talked about how your car will perform like a racecar and perhaps show a picture of someone in a racecar and make the link back to someone's personal car. Or they could talk about the longevity of their tires and how someone will feel smart and will have spent their money wisely. That campaign might be creatively tied to a piggy bank or a wallet. Or they could somehow depict the peace of mind you get with using these tires.

By understanding their consumers' emotional needs and values, and what motivates them, they could choose which of these different campaigns would drive the most response. That's how they ended up with the baby in the tire.

Visually, it looks like this chart on page 111:

The information given to the advertising agency would have been about the family values of its consumers and the higher-order benefit of providing peace of mind because of this terrific steel-belted cable technology. The agency would have taken that information and developed the campaign with the baby in the tire.

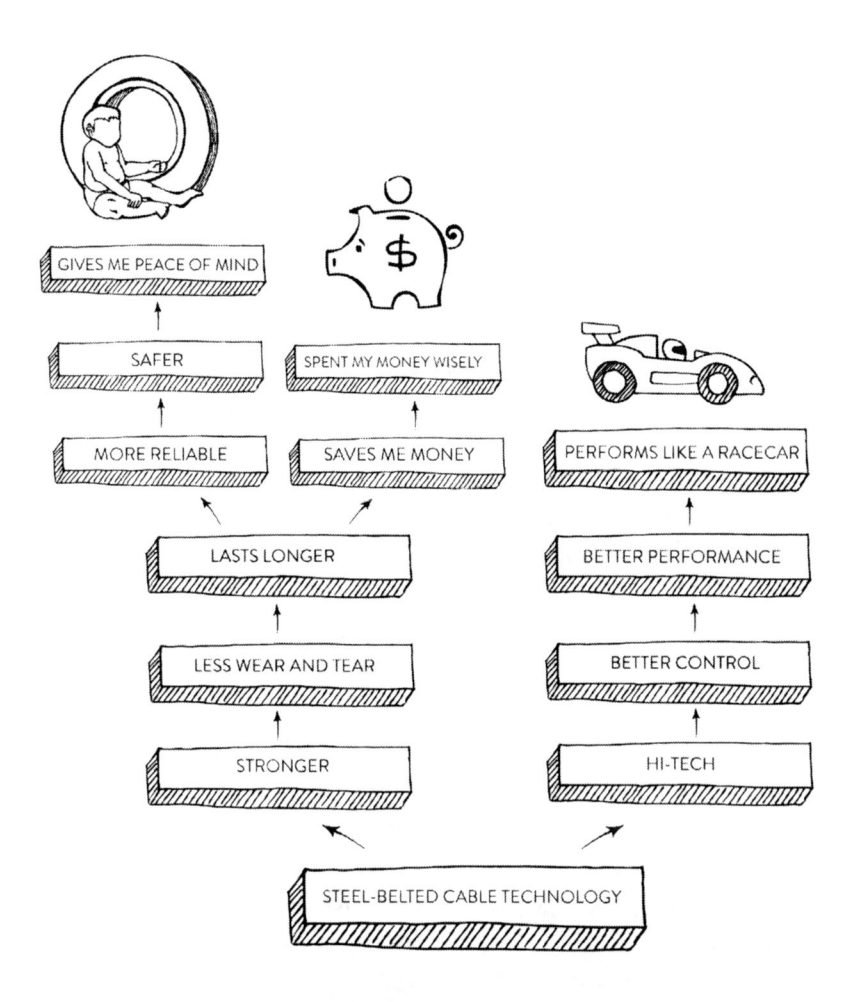

```
GIVES ME PEACE OF MIND
         ↑
       SAFER              SPENT MY MONEY WISELY
         ↑                         ↑
    MORE RELIABLE          SAVES ME MONEY         PERFORMS LIKE A RACECAR
         ↖                  ↗                              ↑
            LASTS LONGER                         BETTER PERFORMANCE
                 ↑                                         ↑
          LESS WEAR AND TEAR                         BETTER CONTROL
                 ↑                                         ↑
              STRONGER                                  HI-TECH
                    ↖                         ↗
                       STEEL-BELTED CABLE TECHNOLOGY
```

Finding Your Unique Higher-Order Benefits

Start with the qualities and skills that you identified in the "Be Clear" chapter, and find the benefits to others of working with you. The trick is to keep asking yourself, "What's so great about that?" This can get really annoying, but it works to push you to a richer benefit that you are uniquely positioned to offer.

We'll use my husband John as an example. For more than twenty years, he has been supporting architects and developers by drawing up construction documents that are extremely detailed. He knows the importance of what he is doing and yet is very humble. He's friendly with everyone, thorough in his work, and draws very quickly. So the qualities that his clients would write about him from the "Be Clear" chapter exercises would be:

- Thorough
- Friendly
- Detail-oriented
- Skilled in AutoCAD® design
- Works quickly
- Easy to work with
- Knowledgeable

To get to his branding edge and turn these qualities into higher-order benefits, he could ask his clients, "What value do I bring to you? Why do you hire me?" The answer to those questions may be higher-order benefits, but they may not be.

And that's the reason for this next exercise. Keep asking the question: "What's so great about that?"

So I'm fast. What's so great about that?

Well, my client can get drawings out faster—especially if they're on a tight deadline

And what's so great about that?

My client will look like a hero to his customers if he uses me as a resource.

What's so great about that?

The client will have happier customers.

What's so great about that?

Word of mouth will grow about my client's business and he'll get more clients.

What's so great about that?

He'll make more money and his business will be more successful.

Visually, it would look like the chart on page 113:

Just as with the Michelin example, you may find that there are several higher-order benefits you could highlight. You may need to talk with your clients or "test" a few of these to see which is most compelling for what you are trying to convey.

Diagram

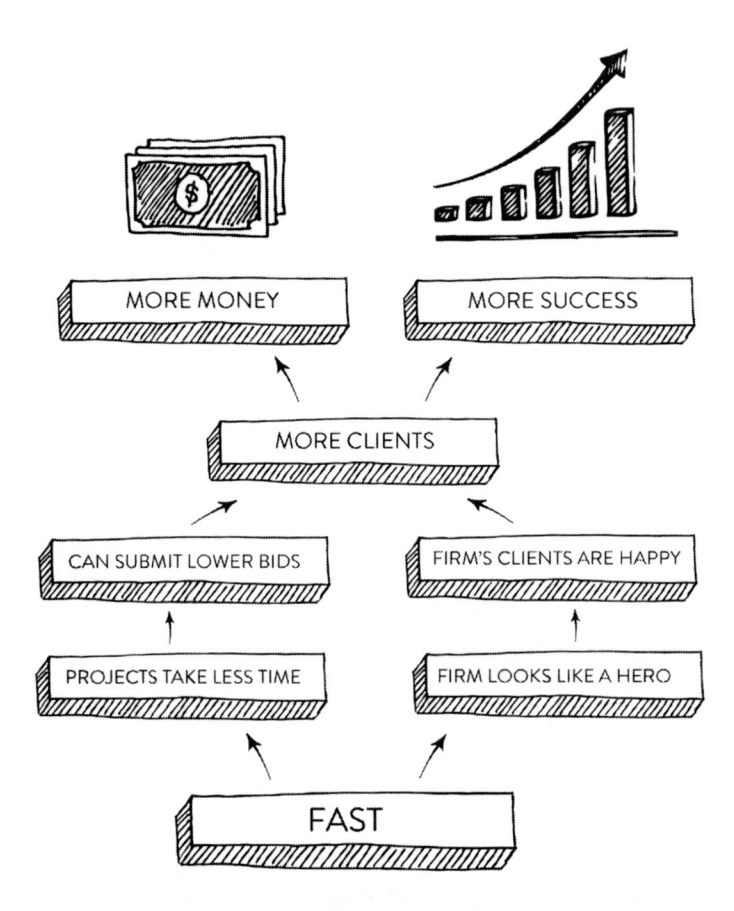

- **MORE MONEY** ← **MORE CLIENTS** → **MORE SUCCESS**
- **MORE CLIENTS** ← **CAN SUBMIT LOWER BIDS** / **FIRM'S CLIENTS ARE HAPPY**
- **CAN SUBMIT LOWER BIDS** ← **PROJECTS TAKE LESS TIME**
- **FIRM'S CLIENTS ARE HAPPY** ← **FIRM LOOKS LIKE A HERO**
- **PROJECTS TAKE LESS TIME** / **FIRM LOOKS LIKE A HERO** ← **FAST**

GET YOUR EDGE

40. Identifying your higher-order benefits

Explore the possibilities for the higher-order benefits that someone might experience from working with/hiring you. Using the laddering exercise, identify some potential higher-order benefits by continually asking, "What's so great about that?" Start by putting your major strengths or skills in the boxes at the bottom of a page, and build from there.

Turbocharging Conversations with Higher-Order Benefits

So how do you use this higher order benefit knowledge in your daily work and conversation? Easy. If John were looking for a job or talking to a prospective client, he could tell them that, if they want to make more money and have happier clients, they should hire him because he's fast, thorough, knowledgeable, and friendly. He would follow up with some signature stories that show those qualities in action and the results someone else has gotten from working with him.

To convey his branding edge, he would talk about projects where he saved his clients time or money, or helped them because of his unique skills. If someone called him on the phone or bumped into him at a networking function or the office coffee room, that person might ask, *"How's it going?"* He could answer, *"Great! I was just talking with my client who had a rush project in order to meet a zoning board deadline. I used this new AutoCAD application that saved us both a lot of time and allowed us to meet the deadline. I was so glad that everything worked out so well for everybody—my client was happy, his customer was thrilled, and I was pleased about the end result. What's up with you?"*

In that scenario, he is not being arrogant or bragging overly much; he's just sharing what's going on in his world (and building his personal brand at the same time). By the way, that scenario shows a good example of a signature story (see page 66–67).

Isn't that more powerful than this conversation? *"How's it going?" "Great! What's up with you?"* If you want to turbocharge your career, then turbocharge your conversations to be bolder in the expression of your personal brand.

Substantiate Your Claims

It is also important to identify why someone should believe that you can do what you say you can do. What is the substantiation for your claims? What are the reasons to believe? When you give a reason for something, people believe you more. So when you develop your proposition and are conveying your uniqueness, you want to provide a reason for them to believe what you are telling them.

This information answers the following questions:
- "Why should someone believe you?"
- "What gives you the right to make that claim?"

In the branding world, people use many different types of credibility components. A company may feature a special manufacturing process, or get a celebrity endorsement to build their credibility. Because Suzanne Somers says that this Thighmaster® works, it must be great, because she has fabulous thighs. Maybe a company tells us about a secret ingredient that makes its cookies more delicious than anyone else's. Maybe a company's leader has a unique business philosophy.

In the personal branding world, you will need to promote reasons for someone to believe whatever claims you are making. If you say you have a certain skill set, give proof of that (maybe it's a diploma or an accreditation you obtained). Sometimes, it's not as tangible as a formal document or degree earned. My husband identified that he has strong attention to detail because of a lifelong ingrained work ethic passed down to him from his mother. You can believe that I know something about marketing because I have more than twenty years of corporate marketing experience with LEGO, Miracle-Gro, Build-A-Bear Workshop, Texaco, and other big-name brands. Those are the credentials I have obtained and those are reasons for you to believe my claims about marketing expertise.

GET YOUR EDGE

41. Outlining your "reasons to believe"

Identify the claims you make from the previous exercises and assign a reason to believe to those claims. Examples include:
- Degree, certifications, or special training
- Awards or honors received
- Number of people, clients, or accounts helped
- Specific experiences
- Time studying or number of years involved in the industry
- Well-known mentor or client
- Someone else's recommendation

Developing Your Personal Branding Action plan

Once you have identified these elements of your personal brand, it should be easy to build an action plan for expressing your branding edge clearly and broadly. The next major aspects of your personal branding action plan is *where and how you are going to communicate your brand*. What specific tactics will you use to turbocharge your career? The overriding message of this chapter is that you need to get outside of yourself and engage with the world around you—the world you want to affect! Anytime there's a project that's relevant to your skill set (or desired skill set), volunteer to be a part of that project. If you have an opportunity to stand up in front of people and talk about whatever it is that you're passionate about, take the opportunity.

So what might my husband have as a part of his personal branding action plan? He could write a blog or an article for a trade publication about the top three timesaving secrets that every architect should know. If he worked in an architectural firm, he could mentor the junior draftsmen (and women) on the proper way to detail a drawing. Each situation would create different opportunities, but in both situations, he could still express his unique personal brand. The key to remember is that his personal branding proposition guides the development of his personal branding action plan.

Be Visible

You must be bold in order to turbocharge your career. I already told you about my victory with numerical analysis. By raising my hand and practicing financial analysis, I strengthened my own personal brand in two ways. First, I increased my skill set, and second, I increased my visibility. Others saw the results of my work, so I became known as someone with numerical skills. In addition, my confidence grew, which led to more leadership opportunities and promotions.

Give Speeches or Presentations

Making presentations is a great way to broadcast your branding edge. Whenever I have a speaking engagement, the audience learns something about me. It creates an impression in their minds about who I am and what I'm all about. So the next time you are asked to present something, say yes. Take advantage of the opportunity to strengthen your personal brand. It doesn't matter what type of presentation it is; it could be a weekly update on

GET YOUR EDGE

How can you find ways to express your brand boldly? The list is endless. Here is a partial list to inspire you:

- Volunteer to lead
- Write an article
- Teach others
- Be a mentor
- Apply for industry awards
- Take someone to lunch
- Speak up
- Give a speech
- Make presentations
- Interact at the office
- Interview someone
- Participate in an online discussion
- Dress appropriately
- Highlight your accomplishments
- Network voraciously

your sales figures, a review of inventory management, or the strategic plan for the coming five years. It could be a presentation to your boss about what you're going to do for the coming week, a status update to your most important client, or an explanation of how you handled a customer complaint. Just realize that it is an opportunity to make an impression. Don't waste that opportunity!

Presentations and personal branding go hand in hand. The last time I conducted a training session for a group of professionals who wanted to overcome their fear of presenting, I advised them to instill more of their personal brands into the presentations. If you do this, you will feel more comfortable with yourself (because you are being authentic), and you will strengthen your personal brand.

Let's say you have a son who pitches in the Little League, and you are also a leader of a lackluster sales team. You need to give a presentation about last month's team performance and motivate them to greater productivity. You could speak about the time when your son was on the mound, throwing ball after ball after ball. Maybe you worked with him, teaching him how to throw, helping him to strengthen his arm. You could talk about how he persisted, not giving in to discouragement, and was able to eventually throw some strikes. You could relate that to how you would like your team to show the same tenacity, the same "stick-to-it-iveness" (or "scrappiness," as my basketball coach would have said) that your son displayed on the baseball field. Your sense of caring and coaching and patience, which are all strong leadership skills, would definitely come through loud and clear. I guarantee that such a speech would be much more motivating than just droning on about closing techniques and meeting quotas, because it will be so much more heartfelt. It will be more aligned with your personal brand and will convey a much stronger message.

If you are terrified of speaking, then practice, practice, practice. I had a client who would give speeches to her daughter's stuffed animals in order to get over her fear of speaking. If you join the Rotary Club, you'll network with people and you'll have an opportunity to stand up every week to talk about something good that happened to you that week.

GET YOUR EDGE

42. Identify your presentation opportunities

What presentations could you make to express your brand more broadly?
What audiences would be interested in hearing what you have to share?
Develop a list of possible presentation topics and venues for delivering those topics. Call and ask someone what the requirements are to make a presentation in that venue.

Volunteer to Lead

In my business, I often work with people who say they want to get promoted. Maybe they are mid-level managers and want to get to the next level. The trick for them here is to find opportunities to lead. They may say, "But I don't have a team to lead. I'm not a leader; that's the whole problem. I want to become a vice president."

You need to find *something* to lead. Maybe it's a project group; maybe you can be in charge of hiring the interns. It might just be one small area, but that's a way for you to prove your leadership, and for people to see those leadership skills. Volunteer to do whatever it is that you want your personal brand to be.

GET YOUR EDGE

43. Identify individual leadership opportunities

What leadership opportunities are there:
- In your professional life?
- In your personal life?

Write

Write about whatever it is you're passionate about. Maybe you're passionate about cost containment, or hang gliding, or mentoring others. Whatever it is in your world, figure out ways to express that. Even sending an email about your passion to five of your friends can have a huge impact. If you make an impression on those five, they may send that message out to five other people who do the same thing. Get your message out there. Be visible.

Is there a topic within your core competencies that might get published in *Business Week*®, *The Wall Street Journal*®, your local paper, the Penny Saver®, your industry publication, or even your own company newsletter? It doesn't matter what it is. If you're interested in it, if you're excited about it, if you're passionate about it, then it is a part of your personal brand. And you can share that passion by writing about it.

Mentor and Teach

You need to share your passion in many different ways. If you teach other people, inevitably they will ask questions about the topic, and I guarantee you will learn even more because you will want to be able to answer those questions. Then you strengthen your brand even further. You can also be a mentor. You will benefit from the exposure and the other person will benefit from your counsel.

GET YOUR EDGE

44. Writing your way to greatness

Think of three article topics you could write about. Write them! Even if you don't know where they will get published, just get started!

Write down a few publications that might be interested in receiving a submission from you. Reach out to at least one of them to find out what format they use to receive that information.

Speak Up

Don't be shy in meetings. Armed with the confidence that we talked about earlier, you already know you have strong contributions to make. Don't assume someone else is going to contribute the ideas. Whatever it is you have to say, say it. Others need to hear what thoughts you have. Remember, you are valuable. You are unique. No one puts thoughts, ideas, and concepts together in the same way that you do. And something that you think is obvious could be a complete revelation to someone else. So have the confidence to speak up. It will strengthen your personal brand.

GET YOUR EDGE

45. Teaching others

Investigate the following:
- Are there any "formal" mentoring or teaching opportunities you could take advantage of?
- Could you volunteer to engage in informal mentoring? How can you make that happen?
- Is there a local college that offers continuing education classes? What could you teach?

GET YOUR EDGE

46. Planning your meeting participation

Take a moment to think about five meetings you participated in recently. Can you identify a time during those meetings when you could have been more vocal?

Think about the next five meetings coming up. What contributions can you make in those meetings? What topics might come up that you could speak to?

Christine's Story—Be Bold

Christine heard me when I advocated being bold. Her early successes came from leveraging prominent placement in a unique way. She reported, "Through my networking efforts, I had the opportunity to design the window treatments for a balcony opening in an upscale, New York–style hair salon that catered to the same type of high-end clientele that I was trying to attract. As an immediate result of that work, I got five new clients who also referred me to others as well."

How does she embody being bold? By always having this question in the back of her mind now: "How can I promote my work through PR and strong word of mouth? Is there a bigger opportunity here?" She once toured the estate of author Edith Wharton and was commenting to the staff about some of the professionally redesigned rooms. When they told her about the top-name designers who had worked on those rooms and their plans for additional future renovations, she asked if she could assist in any future room redesigns; this was met with a positive reaction. **That's** being bold and constantly finding ways to increase visibility. From the moment she moved into her retail location, she made sure that she was very obviously *there*, and she continued to look for ways to be prominent to her target audience. She has been featured in her local paper and posted those articles to her website. Exposure like this had usefulness that extended as a credibility creator on her website.

Christine put a lot of effort into understanding who her clients are. They were not simply high-income ladies who lunch. They were transplanted high-income women who knew what couture windows are and were willing to pay for that extra design sense. Before they would have had to travel to Boston or New York to get the rich fabrics and elegant designs that she provided; they now had a local solution. She was very clear about her unique points of differentiation and what benefits her particular clients received by working with her. She was bold in her pricing because, quite frankly, the high price tag conveyed something more about her brand as well.

Do you know (intimately) to whom you are trying to convey your brand? What do you know about them? Can you profile their activities throughout the day? Are you finding ways to be bold, to be a prominent part of the circles in which they move? Do you know what motivates them? Do this, and you will have a very strong brand indeed.

Get Yourself Out There

Find ways to be bold. Get out there. Be visible. Nobody will know what your personal brand is if you're sitting in your office and just quietly doing your job. A lot of people are shocked that they got laid off. "I thought I was doing a good job!" I hear that so many times. People think it is clearly understood what value they are bringing. I ask them if they did the sorts of activities we are talking about in this chapter and guess what they say. "No, not really. I thought my boss knew that I was good at my job, and that was all I needed to do."

That's not enough in today's world. You want to strengthen your brand if you are in a corporate situation right now. Find ways to express your branding edge—within your department, outside of your department, in the lunchroom, wherever you can!

Network Voraciously

You want to express your brand to as wide an audience as possible, so you want to network voraciously. Meet new people and know you have unique things to bring them. We'll talk more about that in the next chapter, but realize that you need to engage with others who will care about who you are and what you have to say.

If you are an introvert, you may be cringing right now. You may be thinking that you cannot advance your career because you are not outgoing. Take heart; all is not lost. I'm not telling you to be something that you are not. I'm not telling you to go out and stand up in front of crowds of people and shout your message from the rooftops. Remember, I still want you to be true to your brand, which may include a quiet and somewhat reserved demeanor. Everyone can find a way to express who they are, in an authentic way. You can still shine out brightly, even if you are not overtly outgoing. You may not want to give presentations to crowds of people, but that does not mean that you couldn't write an article or engage in a discussion on a blog. Update the status on your LinkedIn or Facebook account, or include a meaningful quote on your email signature. You don't need to do all of these, but you do need to do some of them. Do the ones that match with your personal brand, but do them!

Highlight Your Accomplishments

Remember the strengths discussed in the chapter on "Be Clear?" You need to highlight those strengths and accomplishments to those who need to know what you've done or what you can do. The first step is to think through what those strengths and accomplishments are. Then, look for ways to highlight them. If you are alert for it, you will find opportunities in the course of your conversations to communicate your accomplishments. Remember the example of John and how he could authentically highlight one of his core competencies in a non-sleazy manner. How can you do the same?

In the corporate training workshops I conduct on helping people communicate their personal leadership brands, we practice ways to do this with integrity. I'm not telling you to stand at the water cooler and brag about all the great things you've done. There are subtler, truer ways to highlight your accomplishments. When you love something, you can speak passionately about it. If you're an extrovert, you probably do this already. Often, introverts want to think about a subject first. So, by having already thought about what your accomplishments are and how to concisely talk about your accomplishments, it will be much easier for you to pull those from your memory and relate those skills, those accomplishments, to whatever the discussion at hand is.

GET YOUR EDGE

47. Highlighting your accomplishments

- What ways can you think of to highlight your accomplishments in your everyday life?
- What opportunities do you have to shine a spotlight on those qualities?
- Are there any industry awards you could apply for?

Greater Visibility Can Turbocharge Your Career

An example of gaining greater visibility comes from one of our executive coaching clients who was an assistant vice president of document processing for a leading provider of technology services for financial institutions. Betsy came to me for coaching with a very specific goal. She wanted to get promoted. Betsy was amazing in her job, and, while she loved what she was doing, she was not getting as much recognition within her company as she wanted. She was an innovator who led the way in the "Check 21" legislation-driven image processing revolution that enabled banks and other financial institutions to replace their paper checks with electronic images for payment. This work helped her company become the largest check image processor in her state and the entire region.

Unfortunately, Betsy's was not a high-profile position, and she was not well known by the leadership team. She was a phenomenal leader, her boss thought she was terrific, and the people on her team loved working for her. She had a knack for plucking good people from various areas of the organization and nurturing them to greatness. Her division was the most profitable in the company, but she wanted more recognition for her contributions. In order to do that, and get promoted, she needed to get more senior level exposure.

What She Needed Was Visibility

Being a great employee does not guarantee that you will be promoted, given a bonus, or kept on during a reduction in workforce. That's why you need a strong personal brand. Building a strong personal brand involves looking for ways to spotlight your unique value in the marketplace, and that's what happened for Betsy.

First, you need to know what you are good at. As part of her personal branding exploratory, Betsy identified areas that feed her drive to maximize efficiencies in a company's production areas. "Having gone through this process, I see that my greatest accomplishments have come out of *seeing* innovation and wrapping a business model around that. When you can put efficiencies into production, a company will save money. I get really excited about seeing the solution and then organizing great teams to tackle these big challenges. Now, I'm consciously seeking opportunities to stay on the leading edge of technology to address these efficiency (and profitability) issues in a company's production areas."

The critical step in this process is to shine a spotlight on your personal brand. We put a specific action plan in place to increase the focus on her core strengths, increase exposure at the senior management levels, and highlight her accomplishments in the marketplace. The result? Success! Because she leveraged her branding edge, Betsy was promoted to vice president during the next round of performance management reviews.

One of the contributing factors to her success was a focus on industry awards (this would come under the heading of highlighting your accomplishments). We worked with her company's head of public relations on an awards recognition program. Betsy was nominated, named as a finalist, and eventually recognized at the Connecticut Technology Council's Women of Innovation awards program in the Small Business Innovation and Leadership category for her work on the image processing implementation.

Everybody Wins

By focusing on your personal brand, everybody wins. In this case, Betsy won financially and emotionally, because, in addition to the promotion, she got clarity about the contributions she's making and wants to make every day. Her company won, too, as they were able to harness that passion for the betterment of its clients and its service offerings, as well as earn its rightful reputation as a company that fosters innovative thinkers and industry game-changers. And the industry benefits from the innovation that Betsy and her team are driving.

At the Olympic Games, there are always countless wonderful stories of triumph and trial, of determination as well as disappointment, and it's always fun to watch. Throughout the Games, we get glimpses of an athletes' personal brand and oftentimes those athletes end up on a cereal box after the games. And as a marketer and personal branding expert, I am always asking myself: What lessons can we learn from these athletes? What can we bring to our personal lives as guidelines for living and expressing our own personal brands? How can we stand out in our own worlds?

For those who watched the 2008 Beijing Games, Michael Phelps created a strong personal brand for himself as the most decorated Olympian of all times; he did that by winning over and over again (I would put his efforts in the "Be Professional" category).

One Olympian who epitomizes the concept of "Be Bold" is snowboarding sensation Shaun White. He has a HUGE personal brand (which is one reason he was so *in demand* with sponsors coming out of the 2010 Winter Olympics in Vancouver). One of the interesting aspects of his brand is that fame and glory have come as an after-effect, as a result of his expressing his unique personal brand. If you want an Olympic-sized personal brand, here are some learnings from the half-pipe:

1. *Do your thing.* White loves what he does and does not apologize for that. He works at it. He strives for perfection, innovation, and more! Whatever is part of your personal brand—do it all out. He has found his branding edge and celebrates it in huge ways.

2. *Put yourself out there in a huge way.* Even if it results in a few crashes along the way, you will make yourself known. NBC did a comparison of Shaun White's "air" versus another competitor's air. The difference? At least

five or six feet! How does White stand out? By doing what he does in a huge way. Will he always have a perfect landing? No. But he does everything in a big, Shaun White way.

3. Never be satisfied. This Olympian is always pushing to innovate in this sport. Once outrageous moves are now considered standard. Once that happens, he moves on, looking for new outrageousness—and that marks his personal style. He built his own half-pipe on the side of a mountain so that he could practice new tricks and perfect his moves—over and over again!

4. Continually find new ways to delight your audience. In the Vancouver Winter Olympics of 2010, there was much anticipation about a super-secret new move that Shaun White had been working on that was to be unveiled during these Olympics. In the half-pipe event, each competitor gets two runs and the better of the two becomes the score. White was able to win with his first run (without the new move), so he didn't have to go on the second run. You could overhear the conversation as he was celebrating with his coaches and there was mention of him just sliding down the middle of the pipe. But that wouldn't have been in keeping with his brand! Even though he already had won, he put on a show and performed the new move (even improving on his already-winning score). Ever the showman, White didn't disappoint.

Be bold in the delivery of your brand. It is the crucial step to getting all that you want out of your career. Shine your beacon as brightly as possible so that many can see all the wonderful gifts you have to bring to your world.

Chapter 10

BE DYNAMIC

Branding demands commitment: commitment to continual reinvention.
—Sir Richard Branson, business magnate, billioinaire, founder of the Virgin brand

Kathy Ireland has developed her personal brand dramatically since her days as a supermodel on the sizzling *Sports Illustrated* covers she was famous for in the 1980s. Although in an industry where she was told to "shut up and smile," her passion for business and her design-oriented entrepreneurial spirit would not allow those beach poses to be the only legacy she left to this world. She is so much more than that; she has evolved into the CEO and chief designer for the $2 billion company of Kathy Ireland Worldwide, a company that markets products in a variety of categories around the globe.

Reinventing Her Personal Brand

Ireland reinvented herself by knowing where she wanted to go. She built upon the publicly known image and name recognition she enjoyed in the 1980s to add the previously unknown (but just as ever-present) business savvy with the launch of her company in 1993. She had always been interested in design and business, as evidenced by the painted rocks she and her sister sold around the neighborhood and the newspaper route she maintained (as carrier of the year for several years running!) throughout her childhood. Towards the latter part of her modeling career, Kathy knew these core qualities were already part of her internal brand but she needed to find the right venue to express those qualities externally, in bold ways, in order to dramatically reinvent her personal brand. In effect, she had to expand her branding edge.

Ireland decided to start her new journey with a pair of socks. Because of who she is, you might think that starting with swimsuit design would have been the logical first foray into the design world. But Ireland was concerned if she didn't choose something more drastic, she would never really get beyond "supermodel" status and never be taken seriously as a designer and entrepreneur. It was a strategic, purposeful move to position herself in a new way. Building on the credibility of her name, a sense of business savvy she cultivated throughout her lifetime, rock-solid self-esteem, and an unwavering clarity of purpose unaffected by rejection and ridicule, Kathy Ireland was able to build her company into the $2 billion diversified brand that it is today.

Did her business benefit from her supermodel status and name recognition? Of course it did! This is a smart woman who leveraged what was already known about her to evolve where she wanted to grow. Hers is a perfect example of bold reinvention and constant, purposeful evolution. She analyzed her strengths and weaknesses and put a plan in place to achieve her goals using what she already had.

And you should do the same. You may not be a supermodel, but you still can grow and change and morph into something different. As a matter of fact, you cannot stand still; you *must* evolve. You must grow.

This process of evolution happens naturally. Talk to any 40-year-olds and they will tell you how different they are from when they were 18. That doesn't mean that the skills and qualities they expressed when they were 18 are not still present in their lives, but they've undoubtedly added so many more and are expressing those same qualities in deeper, richer ways.

Imagine how boring it would be if we stayed the same, never growing, never taking on new challenges, never become better people. Throughout your life, you will add new skills and new abilities. We are in a constant state of reinvention. So, why not actively manage the qualities that you're going to bring to your world? You are the pilot of your life. As I have said throughout this book, you are in control of your brand, and you can develop that brand in any way you choose. You need to manage the development and evolution of your brand as purposefully as a brand manager manages the addition of new products to a brand's offerings.

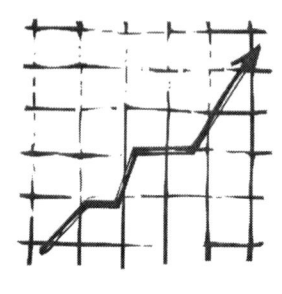

As a brand manager for LEGO toys, I had the responsibility of knowing and holding to the qualities of that brand. Any time a new product was developed, that new product had to fit within the brand personality that already existed for The LEGO Group. LEGO sets are known as high-quality toys, so any new package developed also had to be high quality. For example, it had to withstand certain drop tests so that the packages would not crush in transit to the stores.

When a brand manager says that quality needs to be a part of whatever new offering is being developed, all the developers of that product, the technical engineers, the purchasing agents, and all others involved need to incorporate only designs and materials that are high quality. In this way, the branding becomes a self-fulfilling prophecy. The brand manager demands that quality be part of the product, and those executing have to deliver high quality. Therefore, when that high quality is put out in the marketplace, it reinforces consumers' perception of high quality. It becomes an upward spiral because it's demanded and it's delivered, and, when it's delivered, then the brand becomes known for that quality.

The same applies to you. If there is something you want to be known for, you simply need to start expressing it. It's as simple (and as difficult) as that. Add new qualities to your portfolio. As you start to practice using a particular quality, three things will happen. First, you will become better at that quality; second, people will see that you are expressing that quality; and third, you will become known for that quality.

Explore what it would take to add a new quality. Seek out the advice of people who already have that quality or skill set. Read books or jump on the Internet to learn more about that quality. There is a saying that "Whatever you focus on expands." When you focus on some desirable trait, it will expand because you are focusing on it. In this way, you are in control of your brand. There's no reason for you to be limited in what your brand can be. Be the one who learns to play the piano at age 50. Be the one who takes on a new career at age 40. Be the one who wins a regional award for a new concept.

GET YOUR EDGE

48. The evolution of your brand

> How would you like to enhance or add to your brand?
> What are you afraid of when you consider this?

Actively Manage Your Brand

You are the brand manager of you, and brand managers are charged with growing their brands to increase profitability, grow new markets, and expand the brand. That's what I'm charging you to do. Push your branding edge.

When I was the brand manager for Miracle-Gro plant food, we developed plans to grow the brand. If you are a gardener, you may know about Miracle-Gro. Originally, it was a little box of blue powder that you mix with water and sprinkle over your plants, and it makes your plants look beautiful. This brand is far and away the leader in its category, which is great, but being a heavy market share leader creates different business-building challenges. If you own practically the whole market, you cannot steal share from someone else. So how else can you grow? The answer for us was to enter new markets and to expand the brand beyond its traditional form, beyond the blue powder.

In marketing, the brand itself and the consumers of those brands should guide a marketer's every action. That's why it's so important to understand what a brand is and what consumers think. Companies spend hundreds of thousands of dollars a year to understand their consumers, and that is what we did. We talked to gardeners. And we put a whole bunch of potential gardening products from a multitude of categories in front of those gardeners. "What if we had Miracle-Gro bug killer or trowels or watering cans or weed killers?" The consumers had certain visceral reactions to the products, based on what that brand meant to them. This research enabled us to look at the equity and extendibility of the brand.

The Miracle-Gro brand stands for nurturing and growing, so anything that didn't match up with that (such as Miracle-Gro bug killers) wasn't pursued. Over the next several years, the brand thrived and whole new product lines were added. Miracle-Gro Potting Mix® became a $100 million piece of business within just a few years.

If you want to turbocharge your career, look at what your brand currently is and what you'd like it to be. Find a way to build a bridge between the two!

Build on a Foundation of What You Already Have

So how does that relate to you? You could climb Mount Everest. You could write a book. You just have to ask yourself, "What do I have to start with?" Be guided by what you are now and build upon that. Miracle-Gro didn't try to do everything all at once. They built upon the expanding concept of the brand little by little. Once you develop potting mix, then you can introduce garden soil. And then you can go lots of different places, building upon it in the same way.

This is one of the most helpful concepts in strengthening your personal brand: build a bridge from where you are to where you want to be. This is very empowering and should enable you to use your current situations and skill set and experience base as a launching pad to where you want to be. Apple didn't start with the iPod®; they started in personal computing. The LEGO Group started by selling wooden toys, and BMW® started with airplane engines. In each case, we can look back on the history and see the path that led them to where they are now.

In each case, adversity propelled reinvention and innovation. Perhaps you find yourself currently mired in adversity. If so, take heart from these three examples:

1. After World War I, the German company BMW (Bavarian Motor Works) was prohibited from building airplane engines. The company logically turned to motorcycles and then cars, building its reputation and engineering excellence.
2. The iPad® was a natural evolution. The company expanded on Apple's heritage of simplicity and edgy innovation, evidenced early on with 1984's Apple Macintosh®, with the introduction of the iPod, the iPhone, and eventually the iPad.
3. A Danish wooden toy company established in the 1930s, The LEGO Group experienced a history of several devastating factory

fires that surely influenced family executives early on to embrace plastic alternatives for its interlocking bricks, even in the face of early opposition to plastic toys.

Your Reinvention

What is the foundational path to your reinvention? Those who can see the path that others can't see will get to their destination more quickly. You need to see it for yourself so that you can show it to others. In one of the early exercises, you had to outline a vision for yourself in order to establish goals. If you want to do something different, you need to create that vision for others, help them see how your past is a stepping-stone to the future you are trying to create. In other words, help them see the bridge from *where you are* to *where you want to be*.

So build upon what you have and understand that this activity requires active management. As a brand manager, you can have a five-year plan, a ten-year plan, and beyond that, just as corporations do!

> *In a career, you either go forward or backward; you do not stand still. Every manager must continually improve his or her skills in a lifetime self-improvement program.*
> —Mary Kay Ash, founder of Mary Kay Cosmetics

GET YOUR EDGE

49. Build a bridge from your past to your future

What is the foundation you are building upon? Ask yourself these questions:
- What foundational skills do I have that can be viewed as an asset for the career evolution I am seeking?
- What are the similarities between what I have done and what I want to do. Brainstorm ways to bridge from one to the other.
- What is my five-year plan?

Practicing Versus "Faking It"

Practice, practice, practice. I know I said this in Chapter 7, "Be Professional," but it bears repeating. When people go through training programs, they are advised to try something ten times before they say, "Well, that won't work." If there's a skill you need to master or a strength you would like to add to your personal brand, then you need to practice it. You can become good at anything, but you have to practice.

Have you ever heard the saying, "Fake it until you make it"? I'm not fond of this sentiment, but there is a lesson to be learned in it. If you are trying to be something you do not believe you are at your core, you will not be able to achieve mastery of that skill or quality. You have to add new qualities in your own way, not in a false or phony manner (remember, be true to your brand!). There is power in trying on a new quality and practicing it until it naturally becomes part of your toolkit. If you want to be seen as a more enthusiastic person, practice acting enthusiastic until you feel enthusiastic. I hold a different perspective on that phrase "fake it until you make it." I don't consider practice as "faking it." It is drawing upon a part of you that is already there but is just latent. Think of it as flexing a muscle that hasn't ever really been used before; it's there, but you might not have been aware of it. What you are doing is practicing being something until it becomes so natural to you that you simply do it without thought.

> *The greatest part of our happiness or misery depends on our dispositions, not our circumstances.*
> —Martha Washington, America's first First Lady

My father always told me that "happiness is a choice." I didn't understand that for the longest time. If I was having a bad day, how could I choose to be happy? I now understand that you choose to be happy by *practicing* focusing on the good. This means you don't let a bad mood control you. As I have said before, you are in control. You always have a choice.

Practice Who You Want to Be

Think about experts in their field. Professional ball players practice hitting the ball over and over again until they can do it without thinking. Professional speakers practice in order to be able to speak extemporaneously and naturally. Actors practice improvisation in order to be able to do that well. And in your case, practice being the person you want to be.

I had the privilege of hearing Thurl Bailey speak one time about his basketball career as an amateur at North Carolina State University and then for fifteen years as a professional ball player with the NBA's Utah Jazz. He told the story of his first practice with a new coach (Jim Valvano), who started during Bailey's junior year at NC State. The first thing that Valvano had the players practice was the ceremony reserved for those who win the NCAA championship, the ceremony of cutting down the net and carrying the coach around the arena as a celebration for becoming the NCAA Division 1 Champions. He had them practice winning so they felt like winners. He was helping them to visualize being winners so they could master the skills they needed to be champions. It was this team that experienced the most come-from-behind, unheard of, exciting, down-to-the-wire finish in championship history in 1983 against Houston.

GET YOUR EDGE

50. Practice what you want to be

What do you need to practice?

Practice Confidently

And don't forget to approach this evolution with an innate sense of confidence that you actually *can* master these new skills and add these qualities. While you are "practicing," do it confidently. As I mentioned, these strategies are all interrelated, and confidence is critical.

How would you feel if you were in a hospital and a nurse walked in to your room, looked at your chart, and sheepishly admitted that she was new and didn't really know what she was doing all the while she was doing it. Not too good, right? Wouldn't you rather see a nurse bustle in, check your chart, and do what she needed to do with a smile and good bedside manner?

While you are practicing a new skill, imagine how a master would do it. Let's say you are trying to be more tactful, and you find yourself in a situation that requires tact. Normally, you would simply blurt out whatever comes into your head. But in your evolution, you decide not to do that. Ask yourself, "What would a tactful person say in this situation?" Then do that. In my nursing example, if you were the new nurse, you would ask yourself, "How would a veteran nurse act in this situation?" This technique will speed you along your way to mastery with confidence.

In the Middle of Evolution

Practicing something you are not used to doing can be very uncomfortable. For someone who always has a sour face to concentrate on smiling, it is very awkward and embarrassing. You may feel silly, but do not get discouraged. You are in the middle of an evolution, and that is sometimes difficult.

Don't be too hard on yourself. Change doesn't come overnight. It needs to be practiced daily, weekly, monthly. I've been told that it takes at least three weeks of doing something every day in order to change a habit. Sometimes it takes longer, but remember, you are adding new qualities to something that is already wonderful.

GET YOUR EDGE

51. A safe place to practice

Can you think of a safe environment where you can practice your new skills?

Hard Fun

As a matter of fact, the more difficult the challenge, the more fun it will be. When I worked in the marketing department on LEGO toy campaigns, we often worked with the concept of "hard fun." Hard fun is a vital element of every video, every sport, every board game, every card game, and many toys. Certainly it is a key aspect of LEGO toys.

Everyone enjoys gaining a sense of mastery, a sense of a job well done, a game well played, a challenge overcome, success achieved. Video games provide levels so that you can feel the thrill and the challenge of "getting to the next level." That's an integral part of the fun.

Would you want to play tennis with a two-year-old? Probably not (unless it was your own child or a niece or nephew—and that's a whole different aspect of fun)! You want to be well matched on the court, to play with someone who will give you a run for your money. Even if you are just watching, you want it to be hard on both sides. The nail-biter, down-to-the-wire Super Bowl games are much more fun to watch, even if you are a die-hard fan of one particular team! The triumph is that much sweeter if the challenge is strong.

> *Success is the realization of a worthy ideal.*
> —Earl Nightingale, author and pioneering radio show host

Ever build a LEGO creation? It's not easy. Taking a pile of bricks and turning it into a spaceship or a fire truck or a skyscraper or an alien super-bug takes creativity, thought, and a sense of spatial relations. The pride and accomplishment are integral parts of the fun.

Evolve Slowly

Of course, the trick is to develop something that is hard enough to be a challenge, yet not so hard as to shatter self-esteem. That pride and sense of accomplishment must be there, whether playing a game or building your brand.

As you evolve, make sure you are tackling challenges in a manageable way. When you begin a weight-loss program, they don't tell you to lose 100 pounds all at once. You break it up into more manageable pieces (perhaps two pounds per week) so you can see and celebrate your progress and not get overwhelmed. It's critical to have goals (and they can be really big goals if you so desire) and know where you want to grow. But don't get overwhelmed by trying to do too much all at once. Build a manageable plan to gain a little each day. It's OK to say, "I might not be at top of Mount Everest right now, but that's where I want to get. So what do I need to do to get there? I need to train, I need to learn, I need to climb some smaller mountains and build up to that."

Enjoy the Process of Blooming

As you are learning something new and you feel as though you're just kind of stumbling through, it can be hard to feel accomplished. But I want you to enjoy the process; it's sort of like the age-old advice, "enjoy your childhood." Don't grow up too quickly, because every age is lovely.

Enjoy each stage of development. I often use floral analogies because of my background as brand manager for Miracle-Gro plant food. Think of the evolutionary process as a rose opening. A rosebud is beautiful when it is tightly closed. As that rose begins to open, it's beautiful and magical to see it half opened. When that rose opens and is in full bloom, the sweet aroma is fully released, and that is equally lovely. Each stage of development is wonderful, and there is value in your unique personal brand throughout each stage of your development process.

Don't Compare Yourself to Others

Remember, it's *your* branding edge, not anyone else's. If you had a bouquet of roses that were all tight buds, you would not expect each flower to open at exactly the same time. You would not rip the petals apart to make them open faster—each rose will open in its own right time. One is not better than the other; they are simply opening in their own time. The same applies to you. When you are trying to add new skills or evolve your personal brand, you must be patient with yourself. You will gain skill as you go, in your own time.

Also, understand that one person is a rose, while another person is a lily or a daisy or a carnation. All flowers are different but they are all beautiful.

Continual Improvement

Realize that you are never done. There is always more to do. Keep pushing your branding edge. Each time you achieve a career goal, you set another one! You have a lifetime of achievements to look forward to!

> ### Christine's Story—Be Dynamic
> Christine was continually looking for ways to expand her brand and find more ways for people to engage with her. She added event marketing to her brand-building activities and started offering ninety-minute sewing classes to teach girls the proper way to sew. Christine admitted, "When I first decided to have the classes, I wasn't sure if it would do anything for my business, but I thought, if I don't try, I'll never know." As it turned out, the mom of one of her first students had just moved to the area and needed her entire house redone. By branching out with these classes, Christine found new ways to build her brand by getting the moms in the door.
>
> During one conversation, we were brainstorming ways to expand her business even further, thinking of people she could partner with and other events that she could host in her store. She continually pushed for more innovation in the expression of her brand.
>
> All this effort and focus on developing, refining, and expanding her personal brand absolutely turbocharged her career. At one point, she was asked by another company to be a blogger for them. They were so impressed with what she was doing that they sought her out. So she was be able to add "professional blogger" to her personal brand.

Turn a Negative into a Positive

I find that many people feel inadequate for the dreams they have. They feel their experiences aren't right, their accomplishments aren't big enough, or their networks aren't deep enough. I have to remind people constantly that it is precisely those unique experiences that make them one of a kind. Marketers are always looking for ways to position their products and companies as different, unique, and separate from the crowd. When it

> *In the middle of difficulty lies opportunity.*
> —Albert Einstein, theoretical physicist, Nobel prize winner, father of quantum physics

comes to personal branding, you need to celebrate your individuality, as that is what will make you attractive to the right employer, the right client, the right situation.

I was working with a journalist who had gotten more into public relations and grant writing, but was somewhat timid in expressing these new aspects of her personal brand. She was concerned she didn't have the credentials or years of experience that others in her field had. As I explored this with her further, we discovered that she had a unique perspective on public relations and grant-writing opportunities because of her journalistic background. She said, "I think the PR and the grant writing go hand-in-hand, because I can't tell you how many times I'm working with a client on a grant, and I think of all these PR opportunities. They're just there, and I think of them because I always see the stories, because I think like a journalist."

She didn't need to *apologize* for the journalist background; it was actually a strength! She has been able to expand her brand by using the foundation she had in journalism and writing and add the PR and grant writing to her brand in her own authentic, unique style. This is her branding edge, even though she didn't know it. She could recommend public relations programs because she knows how journalists think. That's the unique talent that she has to bring, and it's up to her to let people know of this talent.

GET YOUR EDGE

52. Celebrate your quirkiness

Have confidence in your singularity. Ask yourself:
- How can I make my quirks work for me?
- How is what I am currently viewing as weird or odd actually unique and compelling, interesting, and different?
- Could something I have been looking at as a negative actually be a positive?

Strengths and Weaknesses: Two Sides of the Same Coin

The journalist's story points out that strengths and weaknesses are actually two sides of the same coin. They are inextricably linked, which can be tricky to manage. You may have noticed that the things you are really great at, the things that make you special, are closely related to what you may also perceive as your character "flaws."

Have you found that to be the case? In my work with executives in many different fields, I have found that this phenomenon is almost always the case. Someone who is detail-oriented can be seen as a perfectionist, someone who is passionate can be accused of being too vocal or fervent, someone who is a creative idea-generator cannot seem to stay on a concept long enough to execute his or her ideas. They are two sides of the same coin.

So what do you do about that?

Well, the first step is to simply be aware of the issue. That's a big step. In actively managing your personal brand, it's critical to know what your strengths are so you can leverage them, highlight them, and build upon them.

But be aware of how that may come across to other people, and how there could be a negative perception associated with it. I have always told people to celebrate what makes them unique; it is what makes them valuable. But be aware there could be some perceived downsides and look for ways to mitigate those downsides. Here I offer two possible solutions:

Compensate with other strengths on your team: If you know that you are a great idea person, but not so hot at follow-through and execution, make sure you have a real go-getter on your team. It can be a beautiful complement to have someone who is not like you on your team. Earlier, I told you about my assistant, Holly. She and I are different—and delightfully so. She is organized, detail-oriented, thorough, task-oriented, steadfast, and patient. I am contained chaos. Having her as a vital member of my team allows me to do what I do best and leverage her most valuable skill set as well. So think about the tasks you hate to do, the ones you don't feel you are good at, and ponder whether there is another team member who would be better suited to those tasks. What qualities would you like to add to your team that may not exist today?

Expand your brand: A major premise of this book is that people can (and do) grow and change. Once you are aware that perhaps you are too

That's not to say there is no merit to looking at your weaknesses and shoring up areas you might be able to fix. However, when we talk about finding your branding edge, we are going to focus on the strengths—maximizing the strengths, and shining a spotlight on the strengths of your brand.

> *God has planted seeds of greatness in every human being.*
> —Mary Kay Ash, advocate for women's business ownership

Where You End Up

When Former Commander of the United States Army and Five-Star General Colin Powell attended Community College of New York, he had a 2.0 grade point average. Now there is a Powell Center named after him. So if you are discouraged about where you are or how you are performing currently, take heart. You are simply on your way to greatness!

Powell believes that everyone can achieve greatness. When he speaks on leadership throughout the country, he admonishes people not to bemoan all the bad breaks they got in life. "Don't go through life looking in the rearview mirror," he says. That's not a quick road to success. Every once in a while, it's important to take stock of where you are and where you've been and celebrate your successes. You may not be exactly where you want to be. You may not have achieved your career and life goals (yet!), but I'll bet you've made progress. Celebrate that progress and keep pushing forward.

Enlist Help

Change is not easy. It can be hard for you, and it can be hard for those around you. One way you can move forward in evolving your brand is to invite others around you to help you change. Tap into your network of supporters to help you. The people who are closest to you can be enlisted in the process. In that way, they will buy in, and they will help you achieve your goal much faster. I'm talking about a spouse, a boss, a colleague at work, or the people who work for you.

The Seeds of Greatness

I have a gardening background, both from spending years as the brand manager for Miracle-Gro and from my master gardener mother, who continues to teach me how to coax loveliness from a bare patch of earth. She was talking about tomatoes, and it reminded me of a very important personal branding lesson.

You see, tomatoes get to a certain point in the ripening process called the "breaker stage," when the fruit begins to turn pink. At this point, a tomato can be taken from off the vine, as nutrients or essentials are no longer being transferred from the main plant to the fruit. As my mother has explained, "The flavor, quality, and nutrition are complete within the fruit."

> *It ain't where you start; it's where you end up, my friend.*
> —Colin Powell, Commander of the US Army Forces, Chairman of the Joint Chiefs of Staff, first African American Secretary of State

The same applies to people and to brands. You are complete and can ripen off the vine. Many of the executives I talk with struggle with self-confidence issues—even when they are in the midst of success! But here's what I have seen. Everyone has what it takes to achieve their goals, if only they will set a plan in place to achieve them.

People ask me how the *Your Branding Edge* program is different from other programs. It's different in that it doesn't just teach theory; it makes people write down a specific plan for how they will express themselves, how they will achieve their goals. Whatever you need to achieve your goals is already within you—whether it is the humility to ask for help from someone who has already traveled down the road you would like to travel, or the patience and persistence to get a meeting with that new client you have been trying to connect with. "The flavor, quality, and nutrition" are already within you.

The same applies to brands. The best new product opportunities and growth development activities come from the foundation of the brand itself. The seeds of greatness are already within the brand. It just needs proper management, strong marketing, and courage to bring that expansion to fruition.

So where is your plan? How are you expressing your brand? What clues can you find in your current brand about how the brand could best be expanded? "The flavor, quality, and nutrition are complete within the fruit (brand)." It's up to you to pluck the fruit and watch it ripen!

What If You Really Screwed Up?

The branding stories we've talked about so far all show how to expand from one set of strengths to another. But what about the disaster stories? One of the questions I'm frequently asked is, "Can you recover when someone has a negative perception about you?" Perhaps you messed up a relationship or handled a situation with a colleague terribly. Can you recover? Yes, absolutely. It may take time and a great deal of effort, but you can change. Lots of people have been able to evolve their brand in spite of negative experiences—in fact, those experiences can contribute to more dramatic growth.

Using a Mistake to Evolve Your Brand

A few years ago, I spoke at a conference where one of Richard Nixon's former advisors, Bud Krogh, was also speaking. Bud Krogh is, unfortunately, known best for his role as the "Plumber" in the Watergate scandal, as he was the first (of many) to be indicted and serve a jail sentence for his illegal actions in that history-altering series of events. But what I learned about Krogh is that he should be known for his moral courage.

He wrote a book called *Integrity: Good People, Bad Choices, and Lessons from the White House*. In it, he talks about his involvement in and the events leading up to Watergate, as well as his resulting growth in moral courage. I highly recommend the book.

My favorite part was when he was in the midst of being tried and had entered a plea of "not guilty due to reasons of national security." He *believed* in what he was doing and did not think he was guilty. During the trial, he had occasion to take his family to Colonial Williamsburg in Virginia. He stood outside the House of Burgesses (the colonial Congress of the 1700s), and pondered all that the colonists had fought for. Among the freedoms vehemently defended by the Founding Fathers was freedom from illegal search and seizure. That's when he realized that was exactly what he had done, all in the name of national security. He had an epiphany and realized that he *was* guilty and needed to go to jail. He changed his plea to guilty and did serve jail time.

Just imagine the moral courage needed to turn around and say, "Yep. I'm guilty. I screwed up, and I should be punished."

The beautiful thing about Krogh's story is that it shows you can change. In my work with people on evolving their personal brands, the topic always comes up, "I can't change. That's just how I am." Here's a perfect story about how you can change in a huge way. Bud Krogh *screwed up in a monumental way*, went to jail, and then *changed in a monumental way*.

He actually only spent 4 and a half months in prison, not that long when you think about it, just one season. Although he was disbarred for five years, it is a testament to his character that he was re-admitted and went on to practice law for many years.

There are many personal branding lessons in Krogh's story:
- If you screw up, you can recover.
- It is possible to learn from your mistakes.
- The terrible things that happen to you can turn out to be the best things that happen to you.

I urge you to read Krogh's story and realize you can *always* evolve your personal brand, adding new qualities and eliminating undesirable ones.

Celebrate Your Evolution

You cannot help but evolve, so evolve purposefully. Determine what you would like to be known for and then go after that wholeheartedly. See every challenge as an opportunity to progress, as a way to add to your brand and evolve your brand over time. Be dynamic. Don't become stale. Add to your skill set and take on new qualities. Take charge of your brand and decide exactly how you want to evolve in order to build a strong personal brand.

Opportunity often comes in disguised in the form of misfortune, or temporary defeat.
—Napoleon Hill, pioneer of personal success literature

Chapter 11

PUTTING THESE PRINCIPLES INTO ACTION

Do or do not; there is no "try".
—Yoda, Jedi Grand Master and member
of the Jedi High Council

You can learn the principles of mathematics, but they will not help you until you apply those principles—to balance your checkbook, figure out your mortgage payoff, or calculate how to send a rocket to the moon. Principles must be put into action.

Whether you are 18 or 83, you need to actively manage your personal brand. If you are at the beginning of a promising career, applying these principles will skyrocket you to success. You will find the shortcut to getting promoted or getting projects that exceed your every dream. If you are at the "twilight of your career," you can use these strategies to continually reinvent yourself so that you remain fresh and alive and relevant your whole life.

Seeing Personal Branding Everywhere

As you move forward, look for examples of personal branding in your life and the lives of others. Think about how they are (or are not) expressing their personal brands and how that is helping or hurting them. Many celebrities are experts at personal branding, and their successes and failures have lessons to teach. For example, Michael Jackson, the self-proclaimed King of Pop, had one of the strongest personal brands of any performer. Here's a guy who was absolutely unique—unlike anyone else. You may love him, you may hate him, but one thing is certain: You know him. You understand who he was, what he stood for, and what he was all about. This personal brand offers a model for anyone looking to present a strong brand to their world:

1. Live Your Talents: Michael Jackson could sing and dance. His branding edge? He was a consummate entertainer and he always did his thing. The lesson? Be what you are. So many people spend a ton of time trying to shore up their weaknesses; stop focusing on that!

Focus on your strengths. Don't try to be an accountant if you don't get excited about numbers. Hire someone who does get excited about numbers. You must find a way to express your own unique talents and abilities.

2. Embrace a Signature Style: Sometimes, something that's a little bit over the top can reinforce and heighten your brand image. For Michael Jackson, the moonwalk and one glittery glove became synonymous with his brand, a part of who he was.

What could signify the type of leader you are? One of the participants in our leadership program is a gentleman with a hard-to-pronounce, hard-to-spell Chinese name of Xingcheng, so he goes simply by "X." To strengthen his personal brand, he has begun to link his name with excellence and execution. It's memorable and effective and epitomizes what his leadership is all about.

GET YOUR EDGE

55. Conveying your personal uniqueness

What's your signature "moonwalk" move?

3. Pursue a Turbocharging Project: When you think of Michael Jackson, you cannot help but think of the music video "Thriller." At the height of the MTV era, this became the quintessential video, a creative triumph that guaranteed him a place in rock history. There have been LEGO minifigure parodies of the song, the *Thriller* dance used as an exercise regimen for prison inmates, and delightful renditions done in my own living room by my 9-year old daughter (twenty-five years after it first went on-air). This is the ultimate example of turbocharging a project in order to turbocharge your career.

4. Love Yourself: One of the great tragedies about Michael Jackson was that he was unhappy with how he looked physically. Over the course of his career, he altered his skin tone and facial bone structure radically. For many,

GET YOUR EDGE

56. Turbocharging your tasks

> What project are you passionate about? How can you take your ordinary project—a routine competitive analysis, your basic marketing plan, your standard corporate event—and turn it into something career defining?

his appearance was never an issue in the first place. We are all our own worst critics. Self-perceived negatives are often only in our own minds and would never be in someone else's minds if we hadn't brought a spotlight on the issue in the first place.

Focus on what matters, the talents and intellectual gifts you've been given. People respond positively to those who are "comfortable in their own skin." If you focus on the value you are contributing, people will accept you as you are.

5. Execute Your Vision: Michael Jackson was undeniably an entertainer extraordinaire. He had a vision for himself and his art that he pursued relentlessly. Find your courage, have faith in your vision, and bring it to fruition. The result could be a lasting icon of business prowess, something everyone refers to one day and says, "That was unique! That's the way to do it. That was groundbreaking."

6. Keep Going: Whether it's big or small, you can overcome any adversity. Maybe you've been fired, maybe you had a disastrous project that went terribly wrong. Whatever career setback you've experienced, don't feel like it's the end of the world. Despite a life filled with controversy, Michael Jackson is still revered by millions. As I said before, I don't care how much baggage you carry about your career. Even a heavily loaded plane can take off. It just needs to begin moving forward.

7. Evolve: There was so much to Michael Jackson's career, from being the youngest of the Jackson Five singing "I'll Be There" to the fashion statement of heavily embroidered, padded-shouldered leather jackets to the ownership of Neverland and his completely sold-out comeback concerts in London, Michael Jackson continued to grow and develop as an artist and as an icon. Evolution is inevitable and desirable. Manage your career and manage the evolution of your personal brand.

Putting the Action Plan in Place

As the brand manager for your brand, you have to put an action plan in place to actively express and evolve your brand. Talk to your colleagues and loved ones about what they think your personal brand is. From that, decide what you like and don't like about your current brand. Decide what you'd like your brand to be. Figure out what steps you can take to add to your brand and get you to where you want to go. Review ways you can be bold in the expression of your brand and decide which ones are most authentic for you.

Developing Your Branding Edge Proposition

This chapter gives you ideas and inspiration for tactics you should consider in expressing your personal brand. However, in order to figure out which tactics will work best for you, you need to start with what you communicate by developing your branding edge proposition. This is a signature statement about who you are and what benefits you bring to the world. It helps clarify for you the essence of what you are and what you have to offer. Your branding edge proposition is composed of five different components:

- Target Audience
- Professional Arena (the category that you serve or the name of your profession)
- The unique benefits you provide
- Substantiation for your claims (the reasons someone should believe you)

Putting It All Together

Once you have identified your target audience, the unique benefits you bring to your professional arena and outlined the most compelling "reasons to believe," you are ready to build your branding edge proposition. Have fun with it! This is a sentence or two that lives in your head and helps guide your career turbocharging efforts! It acts as a filter to weed out people, projects, and companies that will not serve your desired growth, as well as clearly refining the activities that *will* turbocharge your career. It weaves together all four components to ensure that you have captured these major points.

Components of Your Branding Edge Proposition

- Because of (reason to believe), (your name) is the (professional arena) that provides (key benefits) to (target audience).
- To (target audience), (your name) is the (professional arena) that provides (key benefits) because (reasons to believe).

If we continue with John as the example, we might find his worksheet looking something like this:

This takes a bit of time to really get to the point where you are happy with what you come up with. After "noodling" with it for a while, he might have these to choose from (one more conservative than the other).

John's Branding Edge Proposition:

- To architects and developers, John Barthelmess is the trusted architectural resource of choice that frees up your time to go make more money

Branding Edge Proposition Components for:	**John Barthelmess**
Target Audience	• Architects and developers • Construction industry
Professional Arena	• Independent draftsman • Architectural contractor of choice • Architectural teammate/resource • Trusted team member • Architectural secret weapon
Key Benefits	• Allows you to make more money • Gives you peace of mind • Easy to do business with • More time to focus on other areas of your business • Enjoy more success • Deliver work to clients confidently
Reason to Believe	• Old school work ethic • Digital expertise and extensive AutoCAD knowledge • Pleasant manner • Attention to detail • 20 years of experience in residential and commercial architecture

with less hassle by leveraging his twenty years of experience and extensive AutoCAD knowledge.

- John Barthelmess is an architect's or developer's secret weapon to success. His ever-cheerful manner, "old-school" work ethic, and extensive knowledge of AutoCAD make him easy to do business with.

Your branding edge proposition provides the foundation for all your communication—every touch point imaginable. The more true you are to your branding edge proposition, the stronger your brand will be and the more you will turbocharge your communications and, therefore, your career. Let your branding edge proposition become an internal operating manual for all your communications.

Important: Your branding edge proposition is not meant to be an elevator speech or a tagline. It lives in your head only, although an elevator speech or a moniker could be derived from it as a synopsis of your branding edge proposition. If John needed an elevator speech for a networking event, it could sound something like this:

"Hi, my name is John Barthelmess. If you are stressing about getting high-quality, detailed drawings for your client's latest rush project, give me a call. I work independently to handle your overflow projects really quickly so you can confidently go get more clients and make more money."

Adjust for Different Audiences

Please understand that your branding edge proposition may be slightly different for the different audiences you need to target because you will want to highlight different benefits to each. They should not be contradictory, but they can be slightly "skewed" to the person to whom you are directing your efforts. It may be easier for you to break it up into sections. For example, I am a professional speaker and branding strategist at the same time. When I am talking to an event coordinator, they want to know that the audience will be engaged and that my topic will be motivating, whereas a coaching client wants to know that I will help them get results (establish their brand, get promoted, land a job, build their business). In that case, my charts might look something like this:

Branding Edge Proposition Components for:	Rahna Barthelmess Professional Speaker
Target Audience	• Association and company meeting planners • Corporate team leaders • Women's group coordinators
Professional Arena	• Motivational speaker • Leadership training specialist • Personal branding strategist
Key Benefits	• Professional delivery • Dynamic, high-energy presentation • Approachable practicality • High audience engagement
Reason to Believe	• Real-world branding expertise • Published author • Extensive experience sharing branding with thousands in many functional areas (corporate employees, association attendees, entrepreneurs, college students) • Passion for topic • Solid marketing savvy and compelling content • Casual style that puts audiences at ease

My branding edge propositions for these two scenarios might look something like this:

• To those who want to inspire greater team performance and motivate event participants, author Rahna Barthelmess is the professional speaker with more than twenty years of real-world branding expertise to share with audiences to ignite a passion for branding and high audience engagement. Because of her practical marketing savvy and dynamic, high-energy presentation style, Rahna empowers audiences to stand out from the crowd, make bigger contributions now, and map out a path to even greater career success.

• To those looking to turbocharge their careers, Rahna Barthelmess is the personal branding strategist to turn to when you want to grow your

Branding Edge Proposition Components for:	Rahna Barthelmess Branding Strategist
Target Audience	• Entrepreneurs • Sales professionals • Marketing executives • Promotion-minded executives • Job seekers
Professional Arena	• Personal branding strategist • Branding mentor
Key Benefits	• Turbocharge your career • Grow your business • Make more money • Increase your influence • Have more fun in life • Maximize your potential • Achieve greater business success
Reason to Believe	• Real-world branding expertise • Published author • Proven branding process • Experience coaching many types of individuals and companies (corporate employees, college students, entrepreneurs) • Passion for topic • Branding Savvy • Practical application • Individual attention Casual style that puts audiences at ease

business, make more money, increase your influence, and have more fun in life. She has built some of the world's most beloved brands and applies the proven practical real-world branding strategies outlined in her book to impact your brand and help you achieve greater business success.

Developing Your One-Page Personal Branding Action Plan

Throughout this book, you have been analyzing and thinking about yourself, your goals, your desired brand, and the ways that you can bes express and expand your brand to increase your impact on your world. It's time to put all of this into action. Use the convenient workbook sheet to summarize your personal branding proposition and develop your one-page branding edge action plan. Keep it where you can see it and refer to it often. This will help keep it top of mind. It's important to put the best ideas into action right away. There is power in action!

GET YOUR EDGE

57. Develop your branding edge proposition

Gather the most relevant and most compelling information from the previous exercises pertaining to the four proposition components
- Target Audience
- Professional Arena
- Key Benefits
- Reasons to Believe

Develop your branding edge proposition for yourself

You Have Infinite Potential!

There is infinite potential in the seed of a tree. The humble acorn has everything it needs to become a sturdy oak. There is also the potential for an entire forest that, over time, can come from that one seed. And there is the potential in that seed for the beautiful things trees are used for—a tree house, a shaded glen, a fire on a chilly evening. Perhaps the tree will be used to build a house or furniture or a baseball bat or a totem pole; the possibilities are truly infinite. The same is true for you. You have infinite potential and will express a wealth of qualities over your lifetime that will enable you to contribute in myriad ways. Implement the principles outlined in this book and watch your career blossom into a forest of positives—in your life and the lives of those around you.

> *Your real wealth can be measured not by what you have but by what you are.*
> —Napoleon Hill, Advisor to President F. D. Roosevelt

GET YOUR EDGE

58. Building your one-page branding edge action plan

1. Put your branding edge proposition at the top of your one-page branding edge action plan.
2. List your major strengths and attributes and the title of the "signature stories" that embody the expression of that strength or attribute.
3. Write out a 3-month, 6-month and 1-year action plan for the following areas that you can commit to executing:
   - How will you increase your visibility in your world? (presentations, project leadership, articles/blogs, boards/committees)
   - What professional development can you commit to? (training, coaching, mentoring, certifications, books)
   - What networking activities will you engage in? (associations, social media, face-to-face, written, telephone)
   - What aspects of your personal expression will you focus on improving? (office environment, clothes/wardrobe, personal correspondence)
   - What activities will you stop doing in order to turbocharge your career?
   - What other actions will you take to further develop and spotlight your branding edge?

Your branding edge is the key to getting everything you desire for your career. By actively managing your personal brand, you can increase your influence, get a raise, discover massive career opportunities, enrich your relationships, find more joy in your work, and enhance the value you bring to others. Your branding edge truly does have the power to turbocharge your career!

ABOUT THE AUTHOR

For more than 20 years, branding strategist Rahna Barthelmess has passionately built some of the world's most beloved brands, most notably LEGO® Toys, Miracle-Gro® Plant Food, Build-A-Bear Workshops® and Texaco® Gasoline. She understands how to translate classic marketing ideas into practical "how-to's" that people can immediately apply to their own business lives. Rahna pulls from real-life experiences—lessons learned from some of the marketing greats.

As President of Beacon Marketing, Rahna coaches individuals and organizations to help them find their branding edge. Her conversational style and her infectious enthusiasm for branding inspire people to action. And the results? For individuals: careers launched, promotions earned, dream jobs secured. For organizations: double-digit financial growth, 50% increase in client orders, new business goals reached.

Want to engage with Rahna? You can:
- Talk with her via her blog and newsletter
- Work with her virtually via on-line courses or personal coaching
- Book her for an upcoming speaking engagement
- Find her in social media (Facebook, Twitter, Linkedin)
- Meet her in person at a future event

To receive a special guide to personal branding and access the full *Your Branding Edge Success System*, visit: www.YourBrandingEdge.com. To read Rahna's blog and find out more about how to find your branding edge, visit www.YourBrandingEdge.com